# Be Free

## Letting go of the Baggage That is Holding You Back

Dr. Nic Williams

Be Free

Independently Published

Copyright © 2024, Dr. Nic Williams

Published in the United States of America

240903-02569.2

ISBN: 9798304330237

All rights reserved. No part of this publication may be reproduced, distributed, or transmitted in any form or by any means, including photocopying, recording, or other electronic or mechanical methods, without the prior written permission of the publisher, except in the case of brief quotations embodied in critical reviews and certain other non-commercial uses permitted by copyright law.

All Scripture quotations, unless otherwise indicated, are taken from the Holy Bible, New International Version®, NIV®. Copyright ©1973, 1978, 1984, 2011 by Biblica, Inc.™ Used by permission of Zondervan. All rights reserved worldwide. www.zondervan.comThe "NIV" and "New International Version" are trademarks registered in the United States Patent and Trademark Office by Biblica, Inc.™

# DEDICATION

For Lory—

Your unwavering support, resilience, and boundless love have been the backbone of every dream I've dared to pursue, including this one. Thank you for shouldering the weight of our family, for the countless ways you care for our kids and for me, and for embracing this life filled with late nights, early mornings, and endless schedules of church and sports. Your strength and grace breathe life into our home, making it possible for me to follow this call. I know these words are as much yours as they are mine. This journey, these pages, would not exist without you. Know that for every time I don't say it, I still feel it and think it… I love you.

"It is for freedom that Christ has set us free. Stand firm, then, and do not let yourselves be burdened again by a yoke of slavery."
— Galatians 5:1 (NIV)

# HERE'S WHAT'S INSIDE...

| | |
|---|---|
| UNPACKING THE WEIGHT WE CARRY | 1 |
| RECOGNIZING AND ADMITTING YOU HAVE BAGGAGE | 9 |
| UNFULFILLED EXPECTATIONS | 22 |
| UNTREATED PAIN | 38 |
| UNRESOLVED YESTERDAYS | 55 |
| UNHEALTHY VIEW OF SELF | 70 |
| RELATIONAL AND FAMILY BAGGAGE | 89 |
| GUILT AND UNREPENTED SIN | 108 |
| DEPRESSION'S HEAVY LOAD | 124 |
| THE JOURNEY OF ACKNOWLEDGMENT | 142 |
| THE BAGGAGE WE CAN'T LET GO | 165 |
| CELEBRATE RECOVERY: A JOURNEY Of HEALING | 183 |
| LIVING AND CELEBRATING FREEDOM | 196 |
| FINAL REFLECTIONS AND CLOSING THOUGHTS | 210 |
| APPENDIX | 219 |
| ABOUT THE AUTHOR | 230 |

# 1

## UNPACKING THE WEIGHT WE CARRY

It was the fall of 2006, a season filled with anticipation and excitement. Lory and I were newly engaged, and we were in the final stages of planning our wedding. To be more precise, Lory was finalizing all the details while I played the ever-supportive fiancé. My primary task was to plan the honeymoon. After researching all the dream destinations you can think of, we chose Tahiti and Bora Bora, a decision that promised magic and adventure, though that story is best saved for another time.

During our preparations, we realized that neither of us owned any real luggage. We needed something durable, something that could withstand the journey of a lifetime. We went shopping and bought our very first set of luggage: a six-piece set that fit together like a set of Russian nesting dolls. To me, it felt like we had spent a fortune on it, but it was worth it and necessary for the adventure that lay ahead, or at least that's what Lory told me.

Fast forward to today, nearly eighteen years later, and we still have that same set of luggage. It's been with us through countless trips, adventures, international travel, kids, and life changes. However, that luggage is pretty worn out. It's heavy. It has seen better days. Every time we prepare for a new journey, and I grab those bags, I can't help but complain. The baggage is outdated and, in many ways, holds us back. It weighs more than newer models, has only two wheels instead of four, and lacks all the modern conveniences and designs of newer luggage.

Not long ago, as I walked past that old baggage set in our garage, a thought struck me. This baggage was a lot like the emotional and spiritual baggage many of us carry into our lives. It made me wonder. What kind of baggage did I bring into my marriage eighteen years ago that I'm still holding onto today? The truth is, we all carry baggage.

## We all carry baggage

Whether we realize it or not, each of us walks through life with invisible loads that weigh us down, hold us back, and cloud our vision of who we truly are and who we can become. This baggage may look different for each of us: unresolved pain, unmet expectations, guilt, shame, an unhealthy view of self, broken relationships, or unrepented sin. However, no matter what shape or form it takes, one thing is certain: if we don't acknowledge it, our baggage will continue to hinder us from living the life of freedom and purpose God intends for us.

**The Universal Struggle with Baggage**

Have you ever wondered why life can feel so heavy at times? Why is there an inexplicable weight on your shoulders that makes even the simplest tasks seem impossible? You are not alone. Everyone, in one way or another, deals with baggage, those emotional, mental, and spiritual weights that accumulate over time. Some of us carry the weight of past mistakes or the pain of relationships gone wrong. Others are burdened by the relentless pursuit of perfection or the fear of failure.

No matter what your baggage looks like, it's important to understand that carrying it is not a sign of weakness. It is simply a part of being human. Even Jesus invited those who were weary and burdened to come to Him for rest: **"Come to me, all you who are weary and burdened, and I will give you rest." (Matthew 11:28)**. This invitation is open to all of us, regardless of where we are on our journey.

It's not just an invitation; it's a promise. **"It is for freedom that Christ has set us free." (Galatians 5:1)**. I love this verse and find myself sharing it often. At first glance, it might seem redundant, but there's a reason Jesus emphasizes it. He knows that we often don't take hold of the freedom He offers. It's like running into someone who hasn't eaten in days. You go out of your way to buy them some food, only to watch them stare at it, looking back and forth between you and the meal without ever taking a bite, so you say, "I brought you some food so you can eat." It's a simple concept: food for nourishment, freedom for living. However, so often, we find ourselves in a similar situation: offered the gift of freedom by Christ and still choosing to carry the heavy baggage that prevents us from truly living.

**An Invitation to a Journey of Healing**

This book is an invitation. It is not just a collection of stories or strategies. It is a call to take a step: a step toward recognizing and releasing the baggage that holds you back. It's an opportunity to engage in a journey of healing, transformation, and freedom. Each chapter will delve into different types of baggage, from unfulfilled expectations to untreated pain, and will provide practical steps, biblical wisdom, and inspiring stories to help you on your journey.

You will hear stories of people who, just like you, have carried the weight of life's burdens and found ways to release them. These stories illustrate that, no matter how heavy the load, there is always hope for healing and freedom. As you read, you may see yourself in their stories, and you will realize that you are not alone on this journey.

**Why This Matters**

Why is it so important to address the baggage we carry? Baggage is not benign. Left unchecked, it affects every aspect of our lives: our relationships, our work, our self-image, and our spiritual well-being.

Here's the good news: we don't have to carry it alone, and we don't have to carry it forever.

This book is grounded in the belief that God desires for us to live free, free from the burdens that weigh us down and keep us from experiencing His love, grace, and purpose for our lives. **"Then you will know the truth, and the truth will set you free." (John 8:32)**. However, freedom requires a choice, a choice to recognize, confront, and release the baggage that holds us back.

> **Freedom requires a choice, a choice to recognize, confront, and release the baggage that holds us back.**

**Your Next Step**

As you begin this journey, I encourage you to open your heart and mind to what lies ahead. This is not a quick fix or a one-size-fits-all solution. It is a process, a journey that will require honesty, vulnerability, and courage. It will require you to confront things you might have buried or ignored for years.

Take heart. You are not alone. God is with you, and so are countless others who have walked this path before you.

This is your invitation to unpack the weight you carry, to discover the freedom that awaits, and to step boldly into the life God has designed for you. Are you ready to begin?

**Let's Reflect Together:**

- Where do you feel the most burdened in your life right now?
- What might God be inviting you to release in this season?
- How can you start recognizing and admitting the baggage you carry today?
- What has kept you from starting this journey before today?

# 2

## RECOGNIZING AND ADMITTING YOU HAVE BAGGAGE

### The Closet No One Opens

There's a closet in my office that no one opens, not even me. It's the kind of closet you approach with caution, the one where you have to crack the door open just an inch to make sure nothing tumbles out. For over eight years, this closet has been a resting place for anything I didn't know where else to put. Boxes from when I first moved into the office in 2016 still sit there, stacked awkwardly on top of each other. Old files, random equipment, books I've forgotten about, and bits and pieces of things I thought might be useful one day are all crammed into that small space. (I can feel the judgment. Don't act like you don't have a "might use one day" pile.)

I'll be honest. I've attempted to clean it out a few times, but every time I start, I feel overwhelmed. The sheer volume of stuff makes me want to close the door and forget about it. If I'm being even more honest, I might have a bit of a hoarder's heart—I struggle to throw things away. Each item seems to whisper, "You might need me someday," so I tell myself, "Just keep the door shut. Pretend it's not there." Of course, I know it is. In fact, every now and then, something new comes into my life, and it doesn't have a "home," so it gets added to the closet.

Every time I walk by, a small voice in my head reminds me of the mess waiting behind that door. Even though I don't see it, I feel its presence. I know that, sooner or later, I'll have to face it.

Here's the thing. I've realized that the closet is more than just a place filled with forgotten things. It's a metaphor for life.

### Recognizing Your Baggage: The First Step

We all have our "closets," don't we? We all have places in our lives where we stash away the things we don't want to deal with: the hurts, disappointments, fears, and regrets. Just like that closet in my office, these emotional and spiritual clutter points pile up over time, filling our hearts and minds with unresolved mess. And just like I've done with that old closet, we find it easier to close the door and pretend the mess isn't there.

But deep down, we know the truth: if we don't recognize and deal with what's hidden, it will continue to weigh us down, creating an invisible burden that affects every area of our lives.

> **If we don't recognize and deal with what's hidden, it will continue to weigh us down, creating an invisible burden that affects every area of our lives.**

## The Email We Never Want to Open

My wife and I have different approaches to email. If you look at my phone today, I have 110 unread emails. Mostly junk, but I'll thin it out daily. If you look at Lory's phone today, she has 57,328 emails unread. I did not mistype that number. She might have a problem. The truth is, most of those emails are junk and ads. Every now and then, though, some of those emails are important but overwhelming.

Have you ever had an email sitting in your inbox that you just didn't want to open? Maybe it's from your boss, or it's a reminder about a bill you forgot to pay. Maybe it's an email from a friend with whom you've had a recent falling out. You see that email every time you open your inbox, and every time, you feel a slight sense of dread. You think, "I'll deal with it later," but later never seems to come.

Over time, that unopened email becomes more than just a message in your inbox. It becomes a source of anxiety, a nagging reminder of something unresolved. You keep moving it down in your mind, hoping it will disappear, but it never does. Just like those emails, our emotional baggage sits there, always visible in the background, always waiting for us to deal with it. Until we do, it will continue to occupy mental and emotional space in our lives.

## Acknowledging the Baggage: The First Step Toward Healing

Acknowledging the baggage you carry is the first step toward healing. Recognition is not about feeling guilty or ashamed. It's about being honest with yourself and admitting there are things in your life that need attention. In a world that often values appearances over authenticity, it can be easy to hide behind a façade of strength, but true strength comes from vulnerability and having the courage to face the things we would rather ignore.

Think about it. You can't clean a closet without first opening the door and acknowledging the mess inside. Sometimes, that first step is the hardest one to take. It's easier to ignore the clutter, to live with the mess, and to tell ourselves it's not a big deal. However, if we're honest, we know that ignoring it won't make it go away. In fact, it will only get worse.

## The Power of Admission: Liberation Through Honesty

Admitting that you have baggage isn't a sign of weakness. It's a declaration of freedom. When you name your struggles, hurts, and fears, you strip them of their power over you. You create space for healing, growth, and transformation. The Bible speaks to this process of admission and confession. **Psalm 32:5 says, "Then I acknowledged my sin to you and did not cover up my iniquity. I said, 'I will confess my transgressions to the Lord.' And you forgave the guilt of my sin."** The psalmist shows us that there is freedom and forgiveness on the other side of admission. When we stop hiding, we open ourselves up to God's grace and the possibility of a lighter, freer life.

Embracing the act of admission allows us to confront the darkness that we often try to bury. Just as light dispels darkness, honesty dismantles the power of our fears and insecurities. It invites clarity into our chaos. When we acknowledge our baggage, we are no longer prisoners to our past. Instead, we become the architects of our future.

Imagine carrying a heavy backpack filled with stones, each stone representing an unconfessed sin or an unresolved hurt. Every step becomes more laborious, every journey more daunting, but when you finally unzip that backpack and begin to remove the stones one by one, you discover that the load becomes lighter with each admission. **1 John 1:9** reassures us, **"If we confess our sins, He is faithful and just to forgive us our sins and to cleanse us from all unrighteousness."** This is not just a promise. It's an invitation to experience true liberation.

By admitting our struggles, we open ourselves to the transformative power of God's love and forgiveness. It's in this space of vulnerability that we discover the beauty of grace, grace that doesn't just cover our sins but liberates us from them. Having the courage to admit our baggage is the first step towards healing, but it is also the catalyst for profound change in our lives.

As we embrace this journey of honesty, let us remember that we are not alone. The community around us can be a source of support and encouragement. Share your admissions with trusted friends or mentors who can walk alongside you. Together, you can create an environment where vulnerability is met with compassion, and healing can flourish.

> **Admitting that you have baggage isn't a sign of weakness. It's a declaration of freedom.**

### The Fear of Looking Weak

To be honest, there was a time in my life when I believed that admitting my struggles would make me look weak, even if I was just admitting them to myself. As a pastor, I felt the pressure to appear strong and capable, always having the answers and always knowing the way forward. Inside, though, I was wrestling with doubts and insecurities. I feared that if I shared these struggles with others, they would see me as less than, as someone unfit to lead.

One day, a close friend noticed that I seemed burdened and asked if everything was okay. At first, I brushed it off, saying I was just tired or dealing with a busy season. He gently persisted, and something in me broke. I began to share the fears and doubts I had been carrying. To my surprise, he didn't judge me. Instead, he listened, empathized, and reminded me that I wasn't alone. In that moment of honesty, I felt a weight lift from my shoulders. I realized that true strength isn't about never struggling. It's about being honest when you are and deciding to not struggle alone.

**Moving from Recognition to Action**

Acknowledging your baggage is just the beginning of a transformative journey. It's the first courageous step that lays the foundation for true healing and renewal. However, admission alone isn't enough. It requires action to move from recognition to resolution. Just as a builder needs a solid plan before constructing a house, you need a strategy to effectively address the baggage you've identified. This journey can feel daunting, but remember that you don't have to walk it alone. The path to freedom involves practical steps that empower you to confront your past, embrace your present, and step into a brighter future. Here are four essential strategies to guide you on your healing journey:

1. **Seek Professional Help:** Sometimes, recognizing your baggage requires a guide. Consider engaging with therapists, counselors, or psychologists who can offer expert guidance and support. I have been in and out of counseling during different seasons of my life when I just needed a guide to help me process difficult emotions and relationships.

2. **Join a Support Group:** Engage with communities where individuals share similar struggles. Support groups provide a safe space for sharing, understanding, and encouragement.

3. **Practice Self-Reflection:** Invest time in understanding yourself, identifying your baggage, and recognizing how it affects your life. Journaling, meditation, and mindfulness are valuable tools for self-reflection. I have found that being on the water or outside running has given clarity to my headspace that I don't have in my normal rhythm of life. Find what helps you have space for self-reflection.

4. **Engage in Spiritual Practices:** For many, faith and spirituality are sources

of strength and inspiration. Engage in practices that connect you with your faith and spiritual community.

**A Call to Action: Your Invitation to Freedom**

As you move forward, I invite you to consider what baggage you might be carrying. Take a moment to reflect. What have you been avoiding? What needs to be brought into the light? Just like the cluttered closet in my office, which I often ignore, or the emails that linger in my inbox, unresolved baggage can weigh us down, creating a sense of overwhelm. Those unread messages and unaddressed issues accumulate, becoming a burden that distracts us from the present moment.

Recognizing and admitting your baggage is the first step toward a lighter, freer life. It's about clearing out the emotional clutter, just as you would tackle that overflowing inbox, to make space for what truly matters.

You don't have to do this alone. God is with you, and so are countless others who have walked this path before. This is your chance to take the first step toward a life unburdened by the past. Are you ready?

**Reflection Questions:**

- What baggage have you been avoiding or denying in your life?

- How can you begin the process of admitting and addressing that baggage today?

- What steps can you take to move toward healing and freedom?

# 3

# UNFULFILLED EXPECTATIONS

**The Dream Job That Wasn't**

When my friend Mark graduated from college, he had a plan. He was going to land his dream job, climb the corporate ladder, and achieve financial security by 30. He had the degree, the ambition, and all the right connections. When he got an offer from a top company, he felt like everything was falling into place.

However, reality didn't match his expectations. The job wasn't what he imagined. Instead of the vibrant, collaborative environment he had envisioned, he found himself in a corporate maze where creativity was stifled, and innovation was an afterthought. The hours were grueling, stretching late into the night, often accompanied by the unsettling feeling that he was simply a cog in a machine. Every project felt like a race against time, and despite pouring his heart and soul into his work, Mark faced an unsettling truth: he was constantly overlooked for promotions and recognition.

Many of us can relate to the feeling of being stuck in a situation that doesn't align with our dreams. We pour ourselves into our jobs, relationships, or personal aspirations, only to find that the reality is far from the picture we painted in our minds. The initial excitement fades, and frustration creeps in, leaving us questioning our choices. Mark's experience mirrors that of countless individuals who enter the workforce full of hope, only to confront the weight of unfulfilled ambitions. Over time, he became increasingly frustrated, his enthusiasm waned, and he started to wonder where he went wrong. His mind constantly replayed all the "what-ifs" and "should-haves." He had expected to be a success story by now, but instead, he felt like a failure. Every morning, the weight of his unfulfilled expectations hung over him like a dark cloud.

## The Perfect Wedding That Never Happened

Sarah had always dreamed of her wedding day. She had imagined every detail: the dress, the flowers, the music, the venue. It was going to be perfect, a day filled with love and joy, just like the fairy tales she grew up reading. She planned meticulously for months, making sure every detail was just right.

However, on the day of her wedding, everything seemed to go wrong. The weather turned unexpectedly, the caterer was late, and the sound system malfunctioned during the ceremony. What was supposed to be the happiest day of her life turned into a day of stress and frustration. Sarah felt devastated, as if all her dreams had been shattered. She had built up such high expectations that when reality fell short, it felt like a personal failure.

For months afterward, she couldn't help but replay the day in her mind, thinking about how things could have been different. The weight of her unfulfilled expectations stole her joy, and she found it hard to look forward to anything else in life. She realized that her disappointment wasn't just about the wedding day. It was about the expectations she had placed on herself and the need for everything to be perfect.

## The Weight of Expectations: Societal, Familial, Personal

Mark and Sarah's stories aren't unique. Many of us have been there, trapped under the weight of expectations that didn't come to fruition. Expectations are like heavy suitcases we drag through life. They are packed with dreams, goals, and visions of how things "should" be. What happens when those expectations go unmet?

These unfulfilled expectations often manifest in various ways, shaping our identities and influencing our choices. Society imposes timelines. By a certain age, we are expected to graduate, marry, buy a house, or achieve career milestones. The relentless pressure to conform can feel suffocating, as if we're constantly racing against an invisible clock. Our families, too, may have their own aspirations for us, perhaps rooted in tradition or personal experience. They might envision a specific path they believe will lead to happiness and success, adding another layer of expectation we feel compelled to meet.

Then there are the expectations we place on ourselves, the internal dialogues that whisper, "You're not enough unless you achieve this." These voices can be relentless, feeding into our insecurities and self-doubt. They may drive us to pursue goals that don't resonate with our true selves, leaving us feeling unfulfilled and lost.

When these expectations go unmet, they can lead to disappointment, frustration, and even resentment. We may find ourselves comparing our lives to others, feeling like we're falling short. The gap between reality and expectation becomes a chasm that weighs us down, turning our aspirations into emotional baggage that hinders our progress. Instead of moving forward, we often find ourselves stuck in a cycle of striving, overwhelmed by the pressure to perform rather than to simply be.

**The Danger of Unmet Expectations**

Unmet expectations can create a cycle of negativity. We become trapped in a loop of "if only" and "what if." We start questioning our worth, our choices, and our path in life. We can become so focused on what didn't happen that we lose sight of what is happening and what could happen.

Proverbs 13:12 states, "**Hope deferred makes the heart sick, but a longing fulfilled is a tree of life.**" This scripture captures the emotional impact of unmet expectations. When our hopes and dreams are delayed or denied, it can lead to deep disappointment. However, it's crucial to understand that our expectations should not solely rest on our plans or desires but should be aligned with God's greater purpose for us.

God's purpose for our lives is not confined to a checklist of achievements or societal milestones. Instead, it encompasses a beautiful journey of growth, transformation, and connection with Him. The Bible assures us that God has a unique plan for each of us, one that is intricately woven into the fabric of our lives. In **Jeremiah 29:11**, we read, "**For I know the plans I have for you,**" declares the Lord, "**plans to prosper you and not to harm you, plans to give you hope and a future.**"

This verse is a profound reminder that God's intentions for us are rooted in love and a desire for our flourishing.

When we align our expectations with God's purpose, we can begin to see beyond our disappointments and failures. Instead of getting bogged down by what we perceive as setbacks, we can open our eyes to the opportunities for growth and learning that come from those experiences. Each twist and turn in our journey may seem like a detour, but it could very well be a part of God's divine plan, leading us to a place of fulfillment we never imagined.

Instead of allowing unmet expectations to imprison us in despair, we can embrace the idea that God may be redirecting us toward something greater. He is constantly working in our lives, shaping us for His glory and our good. By shifting our focus from what hasn't happened to what God is doing in and through us, we cultivate resilience and hope. It's in this space of understanding that we can begin to cultivate a longing fulfilled, a desire that not only aligns with our heart's deepest wishes but also resonates with God's ultimate purpose for our lives.

## Adjusting Expectations: Finding Freedom in the Present

What if, instead of allowing our unmet expectations to weigh us down, we learned to adjust and reframe them? What if we allowed ourselves to be open to the possibility that God's plans for us might be different, and perhaps even better, than our own?

Adjusting our expectations doesn't mean abandoning our dreams. Rather, it means approaching them with a sense of flexibility and openness. Life is often unpredictable, and the journey may take us through unexpected twists and turns. Embracing this reality can lead us to greater peace and fulfillment. Think about the many times you've set a goal, whether it was to achieve a promotion, buy a house, or start a family. Each goal comes with hopes and dreams, but life can be messy and unpredictable.

> **What feels like a setback can actually be a setup for something extraordinary.**

Sometimes, what feels like a setback can actually be a setup for something extraordinary.

**Here are a few ways to start adjusting your expectations:**

1. **Shift Your Perspective:** Instead of focusing on what you didn't achieve, focus on what you have learned and how you have grown. Life's detours can often lead us to valuable lessons and new opportunities. For example, consider how a failed relationship may have taught you more about yourself, your values, and what you truly want in a partner. Recognizing that these experiences contribute to your personal growth can help you embrace change with a positive mindset.

2. **Surrender Your Plans to God: Proverbs 16:9** reminds us, **"In their hearts, humans plan their course, but**

**the Lord establishes their steps."** Trust that God's timing and plan are perfect, even when they don't match your own. This surrender is not a sign of defeat. It's an act of faith. By letting go of our rigid expectations, we open ourselves to the wonderful surprises that God has in store for us.

3. **Set Realistic Expectations:** Reevaluate your goals and expectations. Are they realistic? Are they aligned with your current season of life? Sometimes, our expectations are based on outdated dreams or external pressures rather than what is truly right for us. It's okay to dream big, but we must also recognize when it's time to recalibrate those dreams. Life's seasons change, and so should our goals. For instance, a recent graduate may need to adjust expectations about landing their ideal job immediately, recognizing that the journey often involves gaining experience first.

4. **Practice Gratitude:** Start each day by listing three things you're grateful for.

Gratitude shifts our focus from what we lack to what we have, helping us see our lives from a place of abundance rather than scarcity. Practicing gratitude can be the secret sauce for finding joy in our daily lives. Practicing gratitude turns what we have into enough. When we actively seek the good, even in challenging situations, we cultivate a mindset that fosters resilience and optimism.

5. **Seek Support:** Don't carry the weight of unmet expectations alone. Talk to trusted friends, mentors, or counselors who can offer perspective and encouragement. Community can help lighten the load and provide valuable insights. Often, sharing our burdens with others opens the door to understanding that we are not alone in our struggles. Connecting with others who have faced similar challenges can inspire hope and reinforce the idea that adjusting our expectations is not only possible but also beneficial.

## The Couple Who Found a New Dream

Lisa and Tom had always envisioned a life filled with children. From the early days of their relationship, they painted a vibrant picture of their future: a cozy home bustling with the sounds of laughter, toys strewn across the living room floor, and family dinners that echoed with chatter and warmth. They imagined holiday gatherings overflowing with joy, where every corner of their home was alive with the spirit of togetherness. However, as the years went by, their dreams began to feel more like a distant fantasy than a tangible reality.

After countless attempts to start their family, they faced the heartbreak of multiple miscarriages. Each loss was like a stone added to the weight they already carried, a weight that pressed down on their hearts and filled their minds with questions: "Why us? What are we doing wrong? Will we ever have the family we dreamed of?" The grief was overwhelming, intertwining with anger and frustration, leaving them feeling isolated in their pain. They watched friends and family celebrate milestones they longed for, and each joyful announcement felt like another reminder of their unfulfilled desires.

Then, one quiet afternoon, after a particularly challenging season, they felt an unexpected, gentle nudge, a soft whisper encouraging them to consider a different path. Hesitant yet hopeful, they began to explore the options of adoption and foster care, stepping into uncharted territory that was never part of their original plan. With each conversation and each new piece of information, they felt a flicker of hope ignite within them. Perhaps there were other ways to build the family they longed for, ways that didn't diminish their dreams but expanded them in ways they never thought possible.

As they journeyed through the adoption process, Lisa and Tom discovered a different kind of family, one built not just on biology but on love, choice, and resilience. They welcomed two beautiful, adopted children into their lives, who brought a richness and depth to their family dynamic that they never anticipated.

Along the way, they also became foster parents, opening their hearts and home to children in need, each child a new thread woven into the fabric of their family story.

Lisa and Tom's journey illustrates a profound truth: unmet expectations can often lead to unexpected blessings. What began as a painful struggle transformed into a life filled with purpose, laughter, and love, elements they once thought were lost to them. They learned that, sometimes, the paths we didn't plan for would lead us to the most meaningful destinations. Their story serves as a poignant reminder that when we release our rigid expectations and open our hearts to new possibilities, we may find a deeper fulfillment than we ever imagined.

> **Unmet expectations can be the starting point for unexpected blessings.**

### Your Invitation to a New Perspective

I invite you to consider what expectations you have been carrying that are weighing you down. What dreams, goals, or visions of how things "should" be are causing you frustration or pain?

As you reflect, ask yourself, "What would it look like to release these expectations and trust God with my future?"

Unmet expectations do not have to define you or your worth. By adjusting your perspective, surrendering your plans to God, and finding gratitude in the present, you can begin to lighten your load and discover the freedom that comes with letting go.

**Reflection Questions:**

- What expectations have you placed on yourself or others that have gone unmet?

- How have these unmet expectations affected your emotional and spiritual well-being?

- What steps can you take today to adjust your perspective and find freedom in the present?

# 4

## UNTREATED PAIN

**Pushing Through the Pain**

"We should run a half marathon together." That's what a few guys on my staff casually suggested back in 2017. Now, here's the thing. I'm not a runner. Sure, I've run off and on throughout my life, but nothing more than a mile or so at a leisurely pace. To be honest, most people who passed me on the road probably wondered if they should stop and offer me a ride. (In fact, someone once did. Thanks, Gary, for believing that if I was running, something must be wrong.) However, as we all laughed about the idea, I realized they were halfway serious.

After some negotiating and perhaps a bit of peer pressure, several of us decided to sign up for a Disney half marathon. Going from not running to preparing for a half marathon required a lot of training. Like Forrest Gump, I just started running, and I kept runnin' and runnin'.

Race weekend finally arrived. By then, some of the staff had wisely decided to switch from the half marathon to a 10K. Being the supportive boss I am, I thought, "Why not run both?" I decided to do the 10K one day and the half marathon the next. In hindsight, this was probably not the best decision I ever made.

Here's the thing about training. When you're preparing for a run, it's usually just you and the open road. There are no obstacles, no distractions, just the rhythm of your footsteps. However, running a Disney marathon with thousands upon thousands of people is a completely different beast. Everyone is an obstacle. As I started running, I got caught up in the excitement of the crowd and ended up starting faster than I had trained for, dodging and weaving through the masses. My adrenaline was pumping, but so were my muscles and ligaments. By the end of the weekend, I had successfully completed both races, but I also had injured myself. I had severe pain on the outside of my knee.

Despite the pain, I found myself hooked on running. I signed up for another half marathon and continued to train once I got home. The pain only got worse. I pushed myself harder, believing I could push through it. I thought if I just ignored it, it would eventually go away, but that pain wasn't going anywhere. It was only getting worse.

Eventually, I had to face the reality that I needed help. When I finally went to the doctor, I realized that if I had seen him sooner, my recovery time would have been much shorter. Now, my freedom to run, my newfound passion, was put on hold because I had ignored the pain for too long.

**The Danger of Ignoring or Suppressing Pain**

My story is a reminder of the danger of ignoring pain, whether physical, emotional, or spiritual. Pain is a signal that something is wrong, a natural mechanism meant to alert us to injury or imbalance. However, many of us try to push through, convincing ourselves it's not that bad or we don't have time to deal with it. We think ignoring pain will make it disappear, but untreated pain only festers and grows, leading to deeper wounds and more significant damage.

In **Jeremiah 6:14**, the Bible warns, **"They dress the wound of my people as though it were not serious. 'Peace, peace,' they say, when there is no peace."** This verse captures a critical moment in the history of Israel, where false prophets and leaders were assuring the people that everything was fine, despite the turmoil and impending judgment surrounding them. This assurance was misleading and dangerous, as it encouraged the denial of real pain and struggle. It serves as a poignant reminder of the consequences of minimizing or ignoring our wounds, pretending everything is okay when it isn't. Rather than addressing the deep-seated issues that plague us, we often settle for superficial fixes or dismissals. This scripture calls us to take our pain seriously, to recognize it as something that requires our attention and healing, not merely to be covered up or dismissed. Just as the people of Israel needed to confront their realities, we too, must be willing to face our struggles honestly, acknowledging the baggage we carry and allowing God's healing to touch the wounds we often try to ignore.

**Understanding the Types of Pain We Carry**

Pain is a universal experience, yet it manifests in various forms that can deeply affect our lives. Recognizing the types of pain we carry is crucial for our healing journey. Here are some of the common types:

1. **Emotional Pain:** This type of pain often stems from experiences such as a broken relationship, betrayal, grief, or loss. It can be the heartache that lingers long after a loved one is gone, the sadness that clouds your days, or the anger that simmers just beneath the surface, ready to boil over. Emotional pain can feel isolating, as if you are trapped in your own sorrow. It may lead to feelings of inadequacy, forcing you to question your worth and your ability to love and be loved. Recognizing this pain is the first step in addressing it. It's essential to allow yourself to grieve and process these emotions fully.

2. **Psychological Pain:** This includes mental health struggles such as anxiety, depression, or trauma. Psychological pain often feels like an invisible weight pressing down on you, making even the simplest tasks feel impossible. It can lead to a sense of hopelessness, where you might feel as if you're trapped in a dark tunnel with no way out. The fight against psychological pain is not just about enduring but seeking help and finding coping mechanisms that work for you. Understanding that these feelings are valid and shared by many can be a source of comfort.

3. **Spiritual Pain:** Spiritual pain arises from feelings of disconnection from God, doubts about His goodness, or struggles with guilt and shame. This type of pain can feel particularly profound because it touches the core of our identity and purpose. You may experience a sense of spiritual dryness, where your prayers feel unanswered, and your faith feels distant. In these moments, it's crucial to seek out practices that reconnect you with your faith community and God, whether

Be Free 43

through prayer, scripture, or fellowship with others who can guide you back to a place of spiritual health.

4. **Unaddressed Wounds from the Past:** Often, pain arises from experiences that were never fully healed. Childhood trauma, a difficult season of life, or a loss that you never fully processed can leave lingering effects that shape your present. These unaddressed wounds can manifest in unhealthy patterns, affecting your relationships and self-image. Acknowledging these past experiences is essential for healing. It may require confronting uncomfortable emotions, but doing so can lead to transformative breakthroughs and a renewed sense of self.

Recognizing the types of pain we carry helps us understand that we are not alone in our struggles. Each type of pain is valid and deserving of attention. By naming these pains, we can begin to address them, paving the way for healing and freedom. It's a journey worth taking, one that leads us closer to the fullness of life that God desires for us.

### The Consequences of Suppressing Pain

Suppressing or ignoring pain can have profound consequences that ripple through every aspect of our lives. Much like an untreated injury that festers beneath the surface, emotional, psychological, or spiritual pain left unaddressed doesn't simply vanish. It often intensifies and manifests in unexpected ways. Here are some potential consequences of untreated pain:

- **Emotional Numbness:** When we choose to suppress pain, we also inadvertently numb our ability to feel joy, love, and peace. The emotional walls we build to protect ourselves can become barriers that isolate us from authentic connection with others. This emotional detachment may make it challenging to engage in relationships or to fully embrace the beauty of life. Imagine a time when you felt overwhelmed by your feelings, only to find yourself withdrawing from those you care about. The vibrant colors of life can fade to gray, leaving you feeling like a spectator rather than an active participant.

- **Physical Symptoms:** Emotional and psychological pain often manifests in physical symptoms that can affect our overall health. Common issues like headaches, fatigue, and gastrointestinal problems can arise as our bodies carry the burden of unprocessed pain. In some cases, chronic conditions can develop, leading to a cycle of suffering that seems unending. For instance, consider how stress from unresolved emotional issues can lead to sleepless nights or a weakened immune system. Our bodies are not just vessels for our spirits. They react to the mental and emotional turmoil we experience.

- **Damaged Relationships:** Ignoring pain can lead to resentment, anger, and mistrust, significantly damaging our relationships with others. When we are hurting, it's all too easy to lash out or withdraw, inadvertently pushing away those we love. Think of a time when you felt overwhelmed and snapped at a loved one. That pain can create a barrier between you and those who care for you, fostering a sense of isolation.

Relationships thrive on vulnerability, and when we suppress our pain, we deny ourselves the opportunity to foster genuine connections and receive support from others.

- **Spiritual Disconnect:** Avoiding the confrontation of our pain can lead to feelings of spiritual disconnect. We might find ourselves questioning God's presence and goodness, struggling to trust that He cares about our suffering. This disconnect can make us feel as if we are wandering in a spiritual wilderness, lost and alone. The weight of unresolved pain can create a barrier between us and God, preventing us from experiencing the comfort and peace that comes from His presence. In these moments, we may feel like our prayers bounce off the ceiling, amplifying our sense of isolation.

Understanding these consequences is crucial for our healing journey. Ignoring pain will only perpetuate a cycle of suffering, while confronting and processing it allows us to reclaim our lives, nurture our relationships, and deepen our connection with God. Only by acknowledging our pain can we begin to move forward, finding the freedom that comes from healing.

**Approaches to Healing and Treating Pain**

How do we begin to heal from untreated pain? The journey to healing can seem daunting, but it is essential for reclaiming our lives and experiencing the freedom that comes from addressing our wounds. Here are some practical steps to guide you:

1. **Acknowledge the Pain:** Just like a physical wound needs to be cleaned before it can heal, emotional and psychological pain must be acknowledged. This means being honest with yourself about what you're feeling and understanding that it's okay to not be okay. Don't dismiss it or tell yourself it's not that bad. Instead, recognize it for what it is: a signal that something needs attention. Allow yourself to sit with the discomfort. It's a crucial part of the healing process.

2. **Seek God's Healing:** In **Psalm 147:3**, we read, **"He heals the brokenhearted and binds up their wounds."** God is a healer who cares deeply about your pain. Take your pain to Him in prayer. Be honest with Him about your hurts and ask for His healing touch. This is an invitation to not only pour out your heart but also to receive His comfort. As you lay your burdens at His feet, trust that He can transform your pain into purpose, helping you find strength in your weakness.

3. **Talk to Someone:** Don't carry your pain alone. Seek out a trusted friend, pastor, or counselor who can offer a listening ear and guidance. Sometimes, just sharing your pain out loud can bring relief and perspective. It's important to have someone who can empathize with your struggles and remind you that you are not alone. Vulnerability can foster deeper connections and create a support system that is vital for healing.

4. **Seek Professional Help:** For deeper emotional and psychological pain, consider seeking help from a licensed

counselor or therapist. There is no shame in asking for help. In fact, it's a sign of strength, not weakness. Professionals are trained to help you navigate complex emotions and can provide tools and strategies for coping and healing. Remember, seeking help is a proactive step toward regaining control of your life.

5. **Embrace the Process:** Healing takes time. Just like my knee injury needed months to heal, your emotional or psychological pain may require time and patience. Give yourself grace and recognize that healing is a journey, not a destination. Celebrate small victories along the way and be gentle with yourself during setbacks. Understanding that healing isn't linear can help you stay focused on the progress you are making, even when it feels slow.

6. **Find Comfort in Scripture:** God's Word is filled with promises of comfort and healing. Verses like **Isaiah 61:1-3** speak of God's desire to comfort those who mourn and bestow a **"crown of beauty instead of ashes."** Meditate on

these promises and let them soothe your soul. Engaging with Scripture can remind you of God's faithfulness and help reinforce the truth that you are loved and valued, no matter the pain you're experiencing.

By taking these steps, you can begin the transformative process of healing from the pain you carry. Each step you take is a movement toward freedom, allowing you to shed the burdens that have weighed you down and embrace a life filled with hope and purpose.

> **Each step you take is a movement toward freedom.**

## Your Invitation to Confront Pain

I invite you to take a moment and reflect on the pain you have been carrying. What hurts, traumas, or losses have you buried or ignored? Often, we think that, by suppressing our pain, we're protecting ourselves from further hurt, but the truth is that unaddressed pain can become a heavy burden, robbing us of joy and hindering our growth. It's time to open the door, let the light in, and allow God to begin His healing work in you.

Consider this: God doesn't promise a life free from pain. Instead, He offers us the assurance that we don't have to face our struggles alone. In our pain, we can experience His presence in profound ways. It's in our vulnerability that we often find the strength to confront the issues we've been avoiding. Just as a seed must be buried in the ground before it can blossom into a beautiful flower, we too, must confront our pain to experience the fullness of life God intends for us.

Remember, pain is not the end of the story. It's an invitation to a deeper relationship with God and a fuller experience of life. By confronting your pain, you are not only acknowledging its existence but also recognizing the opportunity for growth and transformation. Each step taken toward healing is a step toward freedom, allowing you to emerge from the shadows and step into the light of hope and renewal.

As you embark on this journey of healing, know that God is waiting with open arms, ready to meet you in your pain and lead you toward restoration. You are not alone in this process, and it's never too late to seek healing. Take a deep breath, muster your courage, and step forward. The journey may be difficult, but the rewards of freedom and peace are worth every step.

**Reflection Questions:**

- What pain have you been suppressing or ignoring in your life?

- How has untreated pain affected your relationships, health, or spiritual life?

- What steps can you take today to begin addressing and healing this pain?

# 5

## UNRESOLVED YESTERDAYS

### The Echoes of the Past

I remember a day not long ago when I stumbled upon an old journal. It was tucked away in a forgotten corner of my bookshelf, covered in dust and filled with memories I had long since tried to bury. As I flipped through the pages, I saw entries from years ago, moments of joy and moments of deep pain. There was an entry from a particularly tough season of my life in my early 20s. I could see the rawness of my emotions bleeding through my handwriting. Every word was a cry of frustration, anger, sadness, hurt, and loneliness. I had written it late at night, alone in my room, trying to make sense of a situation that had felt so out of control.

As I read through those words, I felt a familiar sting in my chest. I had moved on, or so I thought. Life had moved forward, but the emotions from that season felt as fresh as if no time had passed at all. I realized at that moment that I had never truly dealt with the pain of that time. I had simply tried to bury it, to cover it up, and to keep moving, but here it was again, staring back at me from the yellowed pages of my old journal.

I had spent years carrying these unresolved yesterdays without even realizing it. The truth is that **unresolved pain from the past will always find its way back to the surface.** You can try to bury it, but it will resurface when you least expect it, like a wound that never fully healed.

That day, I made a choice to stop running from my past and finally face it, no matter how painful or uncomfortable it might be.

**The Impact of the Past on the Present**

Our past is a powerful force. The things we've experienced, the hurts we've endured, the relationships that have ended, and the mistakes we've made don't simply disappear with time. Instead, they shape our present in ways we often don't even realize. **Unresolved issues from the past can manifest in various ways.** Anger, bitterness, fear, anxiety, depression, and even physical symptoms like headaches or digestive issues can seep into our present relationships, our work, our ministry, and our spiritual life.

You might find yourself overreacting to a simple comment or avoiding a situation because it reminds you of something painful. You might notice a pattern in your relationships where things always seem to end the same way. Or maybe you feel stuck, unable to move forward, or take risks because you're haunted by the fear of repeating past mistakes. All of these are signs that something in your past is still unresolved.

**Ephesians 4:26-27** speaks to this: **"In your anger, do not sin: Do not let the sun go down while you are still angry, and do not give the devil a foothold."** This verse highlights the importance of addressing our feelings and conflicts promptly. When we let anger fester, we create an opening for negativity to invade our hearts and minds. The devil thrives in this space. He uses unresolved issues to deepen our wounds and amplify our fears, effectively drawing us away from the healing and joy God desires for us.

Imagine your unresolved yesterdays like weeds in a garden. At first, they may seem small and insignificant, but if left unattended, they can overtake the entire garden, choking out the beauty and life that once thrived. The longer we ignore these weeds, the deeper their roots grow and the harder they become to remove. When we hold onto unresolved pain, we risk allowing those weeds to choke out the new growth that God is trying to cultivate in our lives.

By giving the devil a foothold, we inadvertently empower him to influence our thoughts and behaviors, trapping us in cycles of negativity. When we allow old wounds to dictate our present actions, we surrender our peace to the very forces that seek to destroy it. Recognizing this dynamic is crucial. It empowers us to take action. We must actively choose to confront our past and seek healing, knowing that, by doing so, we reclaim our narrative.

Taking control means not allowing our past to write our future. Instead, we can cultivate an attitude of forgiveness and grace toward ourselves and others. This transformation can be incredibly liberating, breaking the chains that once bound us to old hurts and disappointments. Remember, God desires to prune away the weeds in our lives, enabling us to flourish in the present and step boldly into the future He has planned for us.

**Techniques for Resolving Past Issues and Moving Forward**

How do we deal with these unresolved yesterdays? Confronting our past is essential for finding freedom in the present. Here are several techniques to help you navigate this journey:

1. **Acknowledge the Past:** Take a moment to acknowledge what's unresolved in your life. This might mean journaling about specific experiences, speaking openly with a trusted friend or mentor, or simply sitting quietly with God and

allowing Him to bring things to mind. The key is to bring these hidden parts of yourself into the light, recognizing that healing can't happen in the dark. Acknowledgment is the first step toward transformation. It allows you to confront the truth of your experiences instead of living in denial. Remember, it's okay to feel pain, and acknowledging it is a powerful act of self-compassion.

2. **Seek Forgiveness for Yourself and Others:** Unforgiveness is often the root of unresolved pain. Start by asking God to help you forgive those who have hurt you, even if the person who needs forgiveness is yourself. Remember, forgiveness is not about condoning what was done. It's about releasing yourself from the prison of bitterness. One practical step is to write a letter to the person who hurt you, expressing your feelings honestly and openly. You don't have to send it. Just writing it can be cathartic. Then, choose to release that pain to God.

Consider Jesus's words in **Matthew 6:14: "For if you forgive other people when they sin against you, your heavenly Father will also forgive you."** Forgiveness is a choice, a gift you give not only to others but also to yourself.

> **Forgiveness is not about condoning what was done; it's about releasing yourself from the prison of bitterness.**

3. **Reflect on What You Can Learn:** Every experience, no matter how painful, has something to teach us. Ask yourself, "What did I learn from this experience? How has it shaped me?" Reflecting on these questions can help you see past hurts in a new light. Instead of viewing them as failures or wasted time, you can begin to see them as opportunities for growth and learning. Embrace the notion that your past does not define your future. Rather, it equips you with wisdom and resilience that can propel you forward.

4. **Replace Lies with Truth:** Sometimes, our unresolved past is rooted in lies

Be Free

we've believed, lies about our worth, our identity, or God's love for us. For example, if a past mistake has caused you to believe you are unworthy of love, replace that lie with the truth found in God's Word. **John 8:32 says, "Then you will know the truth, and the truth will set you free."** Find scripture that speaks to your value, your purpose, and God's love for you, and meditate on those truths daily. Remember, God's Word is a powerful tool for reshaping our thoughts and beliefs.

5. **Seek Counseling or Mentorship:** If you find it difficult to process your past on your own, consider seeking help from a trusted counselor or mentor. Professional counselors can provide tools and techniques to help you work through unresolved issues. Sometimes, having an outside perspective can provide clarity and healing that you can't achieve on your own. This step is not a sign of weakness. Rather, it's a courageous acknowledgment of your need for support.

6. **Pray for Healing and Release:** Bring your unresolved yesterdays to God in prayer. Ask Him to heal your wounds and release you from the pain that holds you back. **Psalm 147:3 tells us, "He heals the brokenhearted and binds up their wounds."** Trust that God is able to bring healing in areas that seem impossible. Prayer is a powerful way to invite God into your healing process, allowing His presence to transform your pain into hope.

7. **Establish New Patterns:** Identify patterns in your life that keep pulling you back into the past. It might be certain relationships, habits, or environments. Make a conscious effort to establish new, healthier patterns that reflect your decision to let go of the past and move forward. Surround yourself with positive influences and create environments that nurture growth and healing. Change is possible, and as you begin to forge new paths, you will discover the freedom that comes from living intentionally.

By embracing these techniques, you are taking proactive steps toward healing and reclaiming your life from the shadows of the past. Remember, the journey may be challenging, but it is also filled with the potential for profound transformation and renewed hope.

**A Hero's Journey with Unresolved Yesterdays: Tony Stark's Story**

I'm a huge Marvel fan, though I don't always agree with the direction of the franchise. However, since they haven't called to ask my opinion yet, I'll keep those thoughts to myself. One character who has captivated audiences worldwide is Tony Stark, also known as Iron Man.

Tony Stark's story is a powerful example of someone grappling with unresolved baggage. A man of genius, wealth, and charisma, Stark is initially introduced to us as a brilliant but arrogant billionaire, seemingly having it all. Beneath his confident exterior, though, Tony is haunted by his past; his role in the creation of weapons that caused unimaginable destruction and loss. His life is marked by an incessant need for approval, reckless behavior, and a deep-seated sense of guilt and shame for the unintended consequences of his actions.

Tony's turning point comes after he is captured and held hostage by a terrorist group using his own weapons. It's a sobering moment of reckoning. Tony begins to confront the reality of his past choices, realizing that his genius has been both a gift and a curse. The weight of his unresolved yesterdays pushes him to make a dramatic change. Rather than ignoring the pain of his past mistakes, he decides to take responsibility for them.

This decision marks the beginning of Tony's journey toward redemption. He shuts down his company's weapons division and uses his talents to build the first Iron Man suit, ultimately deciding to use his resources and intellect for good. The journey isn't easy. Tony continues to wrestle with his inner demons: his self-doubt, his fear of failure, and his guilt over the lives his creations have harmed.

Throughout the Marvel Cinematic Universe, we see Tony repeatedly confronting his past. He battles villains who are often manifestations of his previous mistakes or creations. He grapples with the consequences of his decisions, from Ultron's birth to the fracturing of the Avengers. However, what makes Tony's story so compelling is not just his struggle but his willingness to face his past head-on.

Tony Stark ultimately finds peace and purpose not by running from his past but by confronting it with courage and humility. (Spoiler Alert) In the end, he makes the ultimate sacrifice to save the world, knowing full well that his past doesn't define him, but his choices do. Tony's story reminds us that redemption often comes when we face our past with courage and commit to change, no matter how painful it may be.

Tony Stark's journey serves as a powerful reminder that we are not defined by our past but rather by how we respond to it. His story highlights the importance of confronting unresolved baggage rather than allowing it to dictate our future. Just like Tony, many of us carry the weight of past mistakes, guilt, and shame. However, it is in our willingness to face these issues head-on that we find the potential for growth, healing, and transformation.

As Tony evolves from a self-absorbed billionaire to a self-sacrificing hero, we see a profound truth: our past experiences, while significant, do not have to limit our potential for positive change.

> **Our past experiences, while significant, do not have to limit our potential for positive change.**

By acknowledging the pain we carry, much like Tony did, we open ourselves up to the possibility of redemption and a new beginning. This requires courage, humility, and a commitment to making choices that align with our values and purpose.

Ultimately, the moral of Tony's story, one that resonates deeply with our own lives, is that healing and redemption are possible. Just as he learned to wield his genius for the greater good, we too, can choose to use our experiences, both good and bad, to foster positive change in ourselves and those around us. We are invited to take ownership of our past, learn from it, and allow it to propel us toward a future filled with purpose and fulfillment.

In doing so, we not only honor our own journeys but also inspire others to confront their pain and seek healing. Just as Tony Stark became a symbol of hope and courage, so can we become beacons of light for those who may still be trapped in their past. Let us embrace the transformative power of facing our history, knowing that our choices today will define our legacy tomorrow.

**Your Invitation: Release Your Past to Embrace Your Future**

As you reflect on your own unresolved yesterdays, consider the cost of holding on to them. How have they shaped your present? What might your future look like if you chose to release them? **Remember, you cannot change the past, but you can change your response to it.**

You are invited to bring your unresolved yesterdays to God, trusting that He can transform your pain into purpose and your regrets into redemption.

**Reflection Questions:**

- What past experiences or hurts do you find yourself holding onto?
- How have these unresolved yesterdays affected your present life?
- What step can you take today to begin releasing your past?

**Action Steps:**

- **Journal Exercise:** Write down a list of unresolved experiences or feelings from your past. Reflect on each one and ask yourself what needs to happen for healing to begin.

- **Forgiveness Practice:** Choose one person or situation from your past where you need to extend forgiveness. Begin a daily practice of praying for the strength to forgive and let go of bitterness.

- **Replace a Lie with Truth:** Identify one lie you've believed about yourself due to an unresolved yesterday. Find a Bible verse that speaks the truth about who you are, and meditate on it daily.

# 6

## UNHEALTHY VIEW OF SELF

### Wrestling with the Mirror

Growing up, I was always my own toughest critic, and much of that came from my lifelong struggle with weight. I remember looking in the mirror, not just to see my reflection, but to inspect every flaw, every imperfection. In high school, I wanted to fit in, to be seen as confident, talented, and put together. No matter how much effort I put into my appearance, my grades, or my social life, I never felt like I measured up.

One vivid memory from my senior year often comes to mind. My friend Jason and I used to ride our bikes around the neighborhoods, both as a way to get around and to battle our weight. However, as much as I tried, I couldn't seem to outrun my food choices. My first-period teacher would bake Otis Spunkmeyer chocolate chip cookies during class. The sweet, warm smell would fill the room, making it nearly impossible to resist. As soon as the bell rang, there would be a line out the door, and I was almost always one of the first to buy a cookie. It was a small moment, but it highlighted a bigger struggle, a pattern of looking for comfort in the very things that kept me from reaching my goals.

I remember a particularly tough day in high school. I had gotten back a test score that wasn't what I'd hoped for, had an argument with a friend, and felt like everything was falling apart. That night, I stared into the bathroom mirror, and instead of seeing the reflection of a young teenager with potential, I saw someone who just wasn't good enough. I didn't see my worth, my value, or the things that made me unique. All I saw were my perceived failures, magnified by the struggles I couldn't seem to overcome.

That night, I made a promise to myself: I would work harder, try more, and push myself to be better. For years, I lived in the shadow of that promise, constantly striving but never feeling satisfied. The truth was I had developed an unhealthy view of myself that would take years to overcome.

It took time, but through a journey of faith, self-discovery, and healing, I began to realize that my worth wasn't defined by my accomplishments, my appearance, or my mistakes. I began to see myself as God sees me: a beloved child with inherent worth and purpose, created in His image.

**Exploring Self-Esteem and Self-Worth**

Many of us have grown up in environments that subtly, or not so subtly, shape our sense of self-worth. From childhood, we learn to measure ourselves against societal standards of beauty, success, intelligence, and achievement. The messages are everywhere: "You are what you achieve," "You are as good as you look," or "You are only worth what others think of you."

It's easy to see how these messages can distort our self-image and cause us to develop an unhealthy view of ourselves. **Romans 12:3**

**(The Message Translation)** puts it this way: **"The only accurate way to understand ourselves is by what God is and by what he does for us, not by what we are and what we do for him."** This verse reminds us that our true worth comes not from external accomplishments or approval but from our identity in Christ.

When we fail to see ourselves through God's eyes, we may fall into various traps that distort our sense of self-worth and lead us away from the truth of who we are in Christ. Here are just a few.

The **comparison trap** is particularly insidious in our society. We constantly measure ourselves against others, whether they are friends, family members, colleagues, or even strangers on social media. In a world saturated with curated images and highlight reels, it's all too easy to feel inadequate. As Andy Stanley aptly puts it, "Comparison is what puts the dis in discontentment." When we focus on how we stack up against others, we become discouraged and disheartened. We often fail to recognize that everyone is on their own journey, facing unique struggles and triumphs. Rather than uplifting one another, comparison can steal our joy and create a sense of rivalry or competition. Remember, there is no win in comparison. It can only lead to discontentment and danger.

The **performance trap** is another way we can misjudge our worth. In this trap, we believe our value is based solely on our achievements and successes. Many of us become workaholics or perfectionists, constantly striving for validation and approval. We tell ourselves that if we just do more, achieve more, or become more, we'll finally feel "enough." This relentless pursuit often leaves us feeling drained and dissatisfied. Instead of finding fulfillment in our accomplishments, we become entangled in a never-ending cycle of trying to prove our worth, which ultimately leaves us feeling empty.

Then there's the **appearance trap**, where our culture places an enormous emphasis on physical appearance, equating beauty with value. We may spend hours obsessing over our looks or feel defeated when we don't meet society's narrow definition of attractiveness. This trap can lead to a distorted self-image, where we feel like we're always falling short, never quite beautiful enough, and perpetually chasing an elusive ideal. The pressure to conform to these standards can be overwhelming and can cause us to overlook the inherent beauty that God has placed within us.

Lastly, the **past mistakes trap** seems to ensnare many of us. We often define ourselves by our failures, regrets, or mistakes. We wear labels such as "failure," "unworthy," or "unlovable," which cloud our vision of who we truly are. When we dwell on what we've done wrong, it becomes difficult to see beyond those moments, leading us to believe we're permanently damaged or flawed. This distorted self-perception prevents us from moving forward and embracing the new life and identity offered to us in Christ.

In each of these traps, we see how the enemy seeks to distract us from our true identity and purpose. By falling into the comparison trap, the performance trap, the appearance trap, and the past mistakes trap, we allow external pressures and internal insecurities to dictate our sense of self-worth. However, when we focus on seeing ourselves through God's eyes, we can begin to break free from these traps and embrace the truth of who we are: beloved children of God who are worthy of love and grace, regardless of our imperfections.

While the comparison, performance, and appearance traps are common pitfalls, they are far from the only ones we encounter on our journeys. In fact, many people navigate a labyrinth of traps that can distort their self-perception and hinder their personal growth. The approval trap, for instance, lures us into seeking validation from others, making us compromise our authenticity in pursuit of acceptance. Similarly, the perfectionism trap sets impossibly high standards, often leading to feelings of failure and discouragement when we inevitably fall short.

Moreover, the victim mentality trap can cloud our perspectives, trapping us in a cycle of blame and powerlessness. We may find ourselves overwhelmed by the busyness trap, mistaking constant activity for genuine productivity and fulfillment. Other common traps include the scarcity mentality, which breeds jealousy and discontent; the isolation trap, where we withdraw in times of pain; and the overgeneralization trap, where one setback leads us to doubt our overall worth.

The **resentment trap** can also take hold as we cling to past grievances that weigh us down and prevent us from moving forward. Additionally, the fear of change trap can keep us tethered to unhealthy situations, stifling our growth and potential. Recognizing that there are numerous traps we can fall into is crucial, as it empowers us to take proactive steps toward liberation and healing. By acknowledging these traps, we can work to break free from the limiting beliefs and behaviors that hinder our growth and embrace the fullness of life that God desires for us.

## Strategies for Developing a Healthy and Positive Self-Image

To cultivate a healthy and positive view of ourselves, we need to confront the various traps that distort our self-image and replace them with God's truth about who we are. Understanding our identity in Christ is fundamental to this process, and here are several strategies to help guide you on this journey:

1. **Recognize Your Identity in Christ:** Embrace the truth that your identity is not determined by your achievements, appearance, or the opinions of others. Instead, it is anchored in who God says you are: a beloved child of God, intricately designed in His image. As **Ephesians 2:10** reminds us, **"For we are God's masterpiece, created in Christ Jesus to do good works, which God prepared in advance for us to do."** Reflecting on what it means to be God's masterpiece can transform your self-perception and inspire you to live out your purpose with confidence.

2. **Speak God's Truth Over Yourself:** Counteract the negative self-talk that often plagues our minds by actively speaking God's truth into your life. For every lie you believe about yourself, find a scripture that speaks truth. For instance, if feelings of unlovability arise, meditate on **Romans 8:38-39: "For I am convinced that neither death nor**

**life, neither angels nor demons, neither the present nor the future, nor any powers, neither height nor depth, nor anything else in all creation, will be able to separate us from the love of God that is in Christ Jesus our Lord."** To help with this, I've included a resource at the end of the book, as well as a downloadable sheet on my website featuring powerful "I Am" statements derived from Scripture that remind you of your identity in Christ. This resource can serve as a daily affirmation to bolster your self-worth.

3. **Practice Gratitude and Self-Compassion:** Start each day by reflecting on the qualities you appreciate about yourself. It could be your kindness, your resilience, or simply your ability to show up each day. Pair this practice with self-compassion. Treat yourself with the same kindness you would offer a friend facing a tough season. Remember, you are a work in progress, and it's perfectly okay to have flaws and make mistakes.

4. **Challenge the Comparison Mindset:** The comparison trap can easily ensnare us, leading to feelings of inadequacy. Instead of measuring your worth against others, focus on your unique gifts and journey. Celebrate the successes of others without diminishing your own achievements. When you find yourself comparing, pause and express gratitude to God for the unique way He created you and the distinct purpose He has for your life.

5. **Seek Healing for Past Hurts:** If your unhealthy self-view stems from past trauma or unresolved wounds, consider seeking professional counseling or therapy. Healing often requires working through pain with someone who can guide you through the process. Remember, there's no shame in seeking help. It's a sign of strength and self-awareness.

> **Surrounding yourself with people who uplift, encourage, and affirm your God-given worth is essential for fostering a healthy self-image.**

6. **Set Boundaries:** Protect your mental and emotional well-being by establishing boundaries with individuals who negatively impact your self-esteem. If someone in your life consistently belittles or criticizes you, it may be necessary to distance yourself or set firm limits on that relationship. Surrounding yourself with people who uplift, encourage, and affirm your God-given worth is essential for fostering a healthy self-image. For further insight into setting healthy boundaries, I recommend the book *Boundaries* by Dr. Henry Cloud and Dr. John Townsend. It offers valuable guidance on how to establish and maintain boundaries that can enhance your relationships and emotional well-being.

7. **Serve Others:** Engaging in acts of service can shift your focus away from yourself and help you recognize the difference you can make in the world. When you serve others, you witness firsthand how God uses your unique gifts to bless and impact lives. This not only

reinforces your value but also fosters a sense of fulfillment and joy that comes from selflessly giving to others. Serving in and through the church provides a wonderful opportunity to connect with community and purpose, reminding you of the collective mission we share as part of the body of Christ.

## Stories of Transformation and Self-Acceptance

Consider the story of Moses, a remarkable example of how God can work through our insecurities. When God called Moses to lead the Israelites out of slavery in Egypt, Moses was overwhelmed with doubt. He stood before the burning bush, his heart racing with fear and uncertainty. Instead of seeing the potential that God saw in him, he fixated on his perceived inadequacies. **"Who am I that I should go to Pharaoh and bring the Israelites out of Egypt?"** he questioned **(Exodus 3:11, NIV)**.

Moses was acutely aware of his shortcomings. He struggled with speech and feared that he would be rejected by the very people he was meant to lead. He could not fathom how someone like him could undertake such a monumental task. His self-doubt became a barrier, clouding his ability to recognize that God had equipped him for this divine purpose. In his mind, he was just a shepherd, a fugitive hiding from his past mistakes, not a leader of a nation.

God saw something entirely different. He viewed Moses not just as a humble shepherd but as a leader, a prophet, and a man chosen to fulfill a divine mission. God reassured Moses, reminding him that He would be with him every step of the way. **"I will help you speak and will teach you what to say,"** God declared **(Exodus 4:12, NIV)**.

Despite his fears and feelings of inadequacy, Moses eventually found the courage to accept God's call. Through a series of miraculous signs and wonders, God demonstrated His power and presence, instilling confidence in Moses. With each step he took, Moses began to see the leader within himself emerge. He confronted Pharaoh, led the Israelites through the Red Sea, and guided them toward the Promised Land.

Moses's journey teaches us that our perceived weaknesses do not define our potential. Even when we feel unqualified or fear rejection, God sees us through a different lens, one filled with purpose and possibility. He equips us with the strength we need to fulfill our calling. Just as Moses overcame his self-doubt and stepped into his role as a leader, we too, can find our purpose when we lean on God and trust in His plans for us.

This powerful narrative reminds us that God often calls us to tasks that seem beyond our capabilities, challenging us to confront our insecurities. With His guidance and reassurance, we can overcome our fears and embrace the unique paths He has set before us.

**Your Invitation: Embrace Your God-Given Worth**

Today, you are invited to see yourself as God sees you, not as the world sees you or even how you see yourself on your worst days. In a world that often measures value by achievements, appearances, or popularity, it can be easy to lose sight of your true identity. God calls you to step away from the comparison, performance, and appearance traps and embrace the incredible worth that He has placed within you.

> **Today, you are invited to see yourself as God sees you.**

You are fearfully and wonderfully made, intricately designed for a purpose only you can fulfill. Scripture reminds us in **Psalm 139:14 (NIV): "I praise you because I am fearfully and wonderfully made; your works are wonderful, I know that full well."** This verse speaks to the divine craftsmanship that went into creating you. Your worth is not contingent on others' opinions or society's standards. It is anchored in the truth that you are a beloved child of God, created in His image.

As you begin to shift your perspective and internalize this truth, it is essential to actively engage in practices that reinforce your identity in Christ. Reflect on the **"I am" statements** from Scripture that remind you of who you are in God's eyes. For instance, you are not defined by your mistakes. Rather, you are redeemed and forgiven (see **Ephesians 1:7**). You are more than a conqueror, equipped to overcome challenges (see **Romans 8:37**). You are loved with an everlasting love (see **Jeremiah 31:3**). These affirmations are not mere words. They are the foundation upon which you can build your self-worth.

Let today be the day you make a conscious choice to embrace your God-given worth. Acknowledge the negative self-talk that creeps in and counter it with the life-giving truth found in God's Word. Surround yourself with a supportive community that uplifts and encourages you. Seek out relationships that affirm your identity and help you grow in your understanding of God's love for you.

In moments of doubt, remember the story of Moses, who, despite his insecurities, rose to fulfill God's calling. Just as he discovered his purpose through God's eyes, so too can you uncover the beautiful potential that resides within you. Embrace the journey of self-discovery, knowing that you are on a path of growth and transformation.

As you take this step forward, trust that God will lead you to a deeper understanding of your worth and purpose. It may not always be easy, but with each step you take, you draw closer to the life of freedom and fulfillment that God desires for you. Go forth boldly, embracing the truth of who you are in Christ, and let your God-given worth shine brightly for the world to see.

**Reflection Questions:**

- What traps have you fallen into regarding your self-worth?
- How have these traps affected your relationship with yourself, others, and God?
- What steps can you take today to start seeing yourself as God sees you?

**Action Steps:**

- **Affirmation Exercise:** Write down three positive affirmations rooted in scripture that affirm your worth in God's eyes. Repeat these affirmations daily.
- **Gratitude Journal:** Start a daily gratitude journal focusing on aspects of yourself you are thankful for.
- **Self-Compassion Practice:** When you notice negative self-talk, pause and ask yourself what you would say to a friend in the same situation. Offer yourself the same kindness.

# 7

## RELATIONAL AND FAMILY BAGGAGE

### The Unexpected Phone Call

Linda stared at her phone as it rang, her heart pounding. She knew who it was, but she wasn't sure if she was ready to answer. It was her sister, Karen, calling. They hadn't spoken in almost two years, and their last conversation had ended in a shouting match at their mother's funeral. Harsh words had been exchanged, and neither of them had tried to make amends. Now, there it was: Karen's name, glowing on the screen.

Linda hesitated, her finger hovering over the answer button. Memories of their childhood flashed before her eyes: playing together in the backyard, secret late-night talks, and sharing dreams about the future. However, the good memories were clouded by years of misunderstandings, jealousy, and unresolved hurt. Family dinners had turned into tense, silent affairs. Holidays were dreaded instead of celebrated. It had been easier to avoid the pain, to let the distance between them grow.

Something inside Linda stirred as the phone continued to ring. Maybe it was the loneliness she felt or the recognition that their fractured relationship was affecting her more than she cared to admit. She knew deep down that avoiding Karen was not solving anything. It was only prolonging the pain. Taking a deep breath, she finally answered, "Hello?"

To her surprise, Karen's voice was soft, almost trembling. "Linda, I've been thinking… Can we talk? I mean, really talk this time?"

That simple question broke down the walls that had built up between them for so long. It wasn't easy. There were tears, awkward pauses, and moments when they wanted to hang up, but for the first time in years, they both spoke from the heart. They realized how much they missed each other and how their unresolved issues had kept them in a prison of pain and regret.

By the end of the call, they hadn't solved everything, but they agreed on one thing. They would try to rebuild their relationship, one conversation at a time. That day marked the beginning of healing for Linda and Karen, proving that sometimes the hardest step is picking up the phone and opening your heart to the possibility of reconciliation.

**Navigating the Complexities of Family and Relationship Dynamics**

Relational baggage is one of the most challenging types of baggage to deal with because it often involves the people closest to us: family, friends, and loved ones. These relationships form the core of our lives. They shape who we are, how we see the world, and how we see ourselves, but they can also be a source of deep wounds, unresolved conflicts, and lingering resentments that weigh us down and hinder our ability to move forward.

Family dynamics are particularly complex. They come with a history, shared experiences, and a web of emotions that are difficult to untangle. You may have grown up with certain expectations or in an environment where conflict was swept under the rug rather than addressed. Over time, these unspoken grievances and unmet expectations accumulate, creating a barrier between us and the people we love. This is what makes relational baggage so insidious. It doesn't just affect one relationship. It can seep into every aspect of your life, affecting your emotional health, your interactions with others, and even your sense of self.

In **Hebrews 12:15**, we are reminded, **"See to it that no one falls short of the grace of God and that no bitter root grows up to cause trouble and defile many."** This scripture emphasizes the importance of addressing unresolved issues in our relationships before they take root as bitterness. Allowing grievances and anger to linger can lead to a festering bitterness that not only harms our relationships but also taints our overall well-being. By confronting our issues and seeking reconciliation, we honor the grace of God and prevent bitterness from poisoning our hearts and interactions with others.

## Tools for Healing and Improving Relationships

Healing relational and family baggage is not a one-time event but an ongoing process. It requires courage, vulnerability, and a willingness to confront painful truths. Here are some tools and strategies to help navigate this challenging journey:

1. **Practice Honest Communication:** Honest communication is the bedrock of any healthy relationship. It means speaking your truth with love and humility while also being willing to listen without judgment. When you open up about your feelings and experiences, you create space for understanding and empathy to grow. Start with statements like, "I feel hurt when…," or, "I've noticed we haven't been as close, and I'd like to talk about it." This sets a tone of openness and encourages mutual sharing.

2. **Seek to Understand, Not Just to Be Understood:** Often, we enter conversations focused on making our own point rather than truly listening to the other person. Practice active listening by asking questions like, "Can you share your perspective on this?" or, "How do you think we can move forward?" By seeking to understand, you show that you value their feelings and are open to finding common ground. This not only deepens connections but fosters a more supportive environment.

3. **Establish Healthy Boundaries:** Setting boundaries is not about keeping people out but about defining what is acceptable in your relationship. Boundaries help protect your emotional well-being while allowing space for healthy connections. Be clear and respectful when expressing your boundaries, like, "I need some time to process before I can talk about this," or, "I'm not comfortable discussing this right now." Healthy boundaries foster mutual respect and help prevent misunderstandings.

4. **Offer and Accept Forgiveness:** Forgiveness is a powerful tool for healing relational wounds. It doesn't mean excusing harmful behavior but choosing to let go of resentment and seek a path forward. As you navigate forgiveness, consider reading *Forgiving What You Can't Forget* by Lysa TerKeurst. This book offers profound insights into the process of forgiving, even when the past feels too painful to let go. Remember Jesus's words in **Matthew 6:14-15: "For if you forgive other people when they sin against you, your heavenly Father will also forgive you."** Forgiveness frees both parties to move toward healing and reconciliation, allowing the relationship to flourish anew.

> **Forgiveness frees both parties to move toward healing and reconciliation, allowing the relationship to flourish anew.**

5. **Pursue Reconciliation Over Resolution:** While resolution focuses on solving a specific issue, reconciliation

Be Free 95

aims to restore the relationship. Sometimes, you may not agree on everything, but you can still choose to respect and value the relationship enough to move forward together. Make the decision to prioritize the relationship over the conflict. This mindset shift can lead to deeper connections and understanding.

6. **Seek Support When Needed:** There's no shame in seeking outside help. Counselors, therapists, or even trusted mentors can provide guidance and support in navigating challenging relational dynamics. A neutral third party can offer a fresh perspective and tools for healing that you may not have considered. Don't hesitate to reach out for this essential support. It shows strength and commitment to improvement.

**Trust that God can bring healing even to the most broken relationships.**

7. **Invite God into the Healing Process:** Remember that God desires restoration and healing in your relationships. Pray for wisdom, strength, and patience. Ask God to soften hearts, open lines of communication, and guide you in each step toward reconciliation. As **Psalm 147:3** assures us, **"He heals the brokenhearted and binds up their wounds."** This imagery reflects God's compassionate role as a healer, tending to the wounds of our hearts. Just as a skilled physician binds up injuries, God desires to restore our emotional and relational wounds, ensuring that we can move forward whole and renewed. Trust that God can bring healing even to the most broken relationships, offering hope and restoration beyond what we can imagine.

**Joseph and His Brothers: A Biblical Example of Reconciliation**

Joseph's story is a powerful illustration of forgiveness and reconciliation, filled with emotional depth that many can relate to. From a young age, Joseph was the favored son of Jacob, showered with love and a beautiful coat of many colors. However, this favoritism stirred jealousy and resentment in his brothers, culminating in a heart-wrenching betrayal. Sold into slavery by those who were supposed to protect him, Joseph faced abandonment, rejection, and the painful reality of being separated from his family.

Imagine the depth of his feelings as he was carted away, stripped of everything familiar, and thrust into a life of hardship. The initial shock would have been overwhelming, leaving him grappling with feelings of betrayal and despair. Each night, as he lay in a foreign land, he must have wrestled with thoughts of why his brothers would betray him in such a brutal way. Those moments of loneliness and uncertainty could have easily turned to bitterness, making it easy for him to hold onto anger.

Joseph's journey didn't end in bitterness, though. Instead, he found himself in Egypt, where, through a series of divinely orchestrated events, he rose to power and became the second-in-command to Pharaoh. God had a plan for Joseph that was beyond his immediate circumstances. When a severe famine struck, his wisdom and foresight allowed him to store up grain, saving not only Egypt but also surrounding nations from starvation.

Years later, when Joseph's brothers came to Egypt seeking food, he faced them once again. This encounter was fraught with emotion. They were the very ones who had cast him into a life of hardship. The memories of betrayal, pain, and isolation flooded back. Instead of seeking revenge, Joseph chose a different path.

He recognized that God had been at work throughout his suffering. In a poignant moment of reconciliation, he revealed his identity to his brothers and spoke these powerful words: **"You intended to harm me, but God intended it for good to accomplish what is now being done, the saving of many lives" (Genesis 50:20)**. Here, Joseph embraced his past, acknowledging the hurt but also understanding how God had used those experiences to fulfill a divine purpose.

Joseph's decision to forgive not only restored his relationship with his brothers but also allowed for the healing of a fractured family. He welcomed them into his life, providing for their needs during the famine and ensuring their survival. This act of grace transformed a painful history into a legacy of redemption, demonstrating that even the deepest wounds can be healed with God's help.

His story reminds us that while relational baggage can weigh us down, it can also become a testimony of God's faithfulness. Just as Joseph overcame the pain inflicted by his brothers, we too, can choose the path of forgiveness, allowing God to turn our trials into triumphs. Through Joseph's journey, we see that our past does not have to define our future. Instead, it can be a catalyst for God's purpose and healing in our lives.

**A Contemporary Story of Reconciliation: Mary and Her Mother**

Mary had always had a strained relationship with her mother, Jane. Growing up, she felt like she could never meet her mother's high expectations, leading to a constant feeling of inadequacy and resentment. Jane, on the other hand, felt misunderstood and hurt by what she saw as Mary's rebellion and rejection. Their relationship became a cycle of criticism and defense, each misunderstanding deepening the chasm between them.

Years went by, and their communication dwindled to rare, superficial phone calls. Mary often found herself longing for a closer relationship with her mother, but she didn't know how to bridge the gap. One day, after a particularly moving church service, she felt a nudge in her heart to reach out.

She sent a simple text: *Mom, can we talk? I miss you.* Jane replied almost immediately, agreeing to meet. When they sat down together, Mary felt nervous, unsure how the conversation would go, but she decided to be honest about her feelings without blaming her mother. She said, "Mom, I know we haven't always seen eye to eye, but I want to understand you better. I feel like I've never really listened to your side."

Jane, taken aback by Mary's openness, started to share her own feelings of hurt and fear. For the first time, they listened to each other without interrupting or defending. Tears flowed as they realized how much pain they had both been carrying. It wasn't an instant fix, but it was a start. They committed to rebuilding their relationship, one honest conversation at a time.

**Your Invitation: Release and Reconcile**

Relational and family baggage can feel like a heavy weight, but it doesn't have to define you or your future. Each of us carries experiences, wounds, and stories that shape our relationships. The beauty of God's grace is that it offers us the opportunity to transform those burdens into pathways for healing and connection.

You are invited to take the first step in seeking healing, which may mean confronting uncomfortable truths or initiating difficult conversations. This journey begins with acknowledging the pain and allowing yourself to feel the emotions tied to those experiences. It's a courageous act to face what has been buried, and it can lead to profound personal growth.

Setting healthy boundaries is another essential aspect of this process. Boundaries are not about shutting others out. They are about defining what is acceptable in your relationships and protecting your emotional well-being. Establishing boundaries can help create a safe space where relationships can flourish without the weight of unresolved issues hanging over them.

Extending grace to yourself is equally important. Many of us are our own harshest critics, often holding onto guilt or shame for past mistakes. Remember that you deserve the same compassion you would offer to a friend. Allow yourself the grace to heal, learn, and grow from your experiences. Forgiveness, both for yourself and for others, can be a liberating step toward reconciliation.

Throughout this journey, keep in mind that God is with you in this process. His heart is for reconciliation and restoration. He understands the complexity of your relationships and desires to guide you through the healing process. Lean into His presence through prayer, asking for strength, wisdom, and the courage to take the necessary steps toward healing.

As you embark on this journey, trust that each step you take brings you closer to freedom and wholeness. The weight of relational baggage can be lifted, allowing you to embrace the fullness of life that God has intended for you. Choose to release what no longer serves you and open your heart to the possibilities of renewed relationships.

Remember, healing is not just about letting go; it's about growing into the person God has called you to be. It's a process that takes time, but with patience and perseverance, you can find a renewed sense of peace, joy, and connection in your relationships. Embrace this invitation to release and reconcile, and watch as God transforms your past pain into a powerful testimony of His grace and love.

**Reflection Questions:**

- Are there any relationships in your life that are strained or broken?
- What steps can you take today to begin healing and reconciliation in these relationships?
- How can you invite God into this process of healing?
- What boundaries do you need to set to protect your emotional well-being while pursuing reconciliation?
- How can you practice self-compassion as you navigate these challenging relationships?

**Action Steps:**

- **Write a Letter:** If you find it difficult to speak directly, write a letter to the person with whom you have unresolved issues. Express your feelings honestly and share your desire for healing and reconciliation. This can be a cathartic exercise that helps you clarify your thoughts and feelings.

- **Pray for Healing:** Make a list of the people you have strained relationships with and commit to praying for them regularly. Ask God to soften your heart, guide your interactions, and bring healing to those relationships.

- **Reach Out for a Conversation:** After reflecting and praying, consider reaching out to the person with whom you want to reconcile. Initiate a conversation where both of you can express your feelings and work toward understanding one another better.

- **Establish Boundaries:** Identify any toxic dynamics in your relationships. Set clear boundaries that protect your emotional health while still allowing for reconciliation. Communicate these boundaries kindly but firmly.

- **Engage in Acts of Kindness:** Demonstrate your commitment to reconciliation by performing small acts of kindness for the person involved. This can help rebuild trust and open the door to more positive interactions.

- **Seek Guidance:** Consider talking to a trusted mentor, counselor, or pastor about your desire to heal these relationships. Their perspective and advice can provide valuable insights and support as you navigate this journey.

# 8

## GUILT AND UNREPENTED SIN

**The Heavy Weight of Regret**

Michael sat in his car, gripping the steering wheel tightly, staring blankly at the parking lot outside his office. He had just finished another long, exhausting day at work, but he couldn't bring himself to turn the key in the ignition and head home. It wasn't because of traffic or bad weather. It was because of the overwhelming weight he felt pressing down on his chest, a weight that had grown heavier each day for the past few years.

Three years ago, Michael made a decision that changed his life forever. He had betrayed a close friend, a man who had trusted him, by spreading a rumor that was both false and damaging. At the time, he had acted out of jealousy and spite, wanting to feel important in a circle of friends who seemed to admire his friend more than him. The fallout was swift. His friend's reputation was shattered, relationships were fractured, and Michael was left with a deep sense of regret and guilt.

For a while, he convinced himself it was no big deal, that everyone made mistakes and moved on, but guilt has a way of lingering, festering in the hidden corners of the heart. Michael found himself replaying that moment in his mind over and over again, feeling the shame and remorse build with each passing day. He felt trapped, unable to move forward, constantly haunted by what he had done.

One night, as he sat in his car, his eyes filled with tears. He whispered a prayer, "God, I don't know how to move past this. I don't know how to forgive myself. Please help me find a way to let go of this guilt."

## Understanding and Addressing Guilt and Sin

Guilt is an emotion we all experience at some point in our lives. It often arises when we've done something we know is wrong, hurt someone, or acted against our own values. Guilt, when left unaddressed, can become a heavy burden that hinders us from moving forward. It can rob us of joy, peace, and the ability to live fully.

Guilt doesn't always have to be negative, however. In its healthy form, guilt can act as a catalyst for change, prompting us to seek forgiveness, make amends, and grow from our mistakes. The problem arises when guilt becomes toxic, when we hold onto it, allowing it to define us, or when we refuse to acknowledge it and instead bury it deep within ourselves.

Living in Florida, I can relate to the feeling of being completely sapped by the heat of the summer. The oppressive humidity and sweltering temperatures can drain your energy, leaving you feeling sluggish and overwhelmed. This physical sensation mirrors the emotional and spiritual weight we carry when we keep silent about our struggles or refuse to address our sins.

**Psalm 32:3-4** speaks to this profound truth: **"When I kept silent, my bones wasted away through my groaning all day long. For day and night your hand was heavy on me; my strength was sapped as in the heat of summer."** This powerful verse encapsulates the toll that unrepented sin takes on our bodies and souls. Just as the relentless heat of a Florida summer can leave us parched and depleted, so too can unresolved sin and unconfessed struggles drain our emotional and spiritual vitality.

The imagery here is striking. When we choose silence over confession, we risk allowing guilt and shame to fester within us, manifesting as physical ailments and emotional burdens. The pressure builds until it feels unbearable, much like the oppressive summer heat that weighs down on us relentlessly. However, the beauty of this scripture also points to the promise of relief. Just as a summer storm can bring much-needed rain to cool the parched earth, so confession and repentance can lead to healing and restoration.

By acknowledging our struggles and bringing them before God, we open ourselves to His grace and mercy.

> **By acknowledging our struggles and bringing them before God, we open ourselves to His grace and mercy.**

The act of confession not only lightens our burdens but also revitalizes our spirits. It allows us to release the weight of guilt and step into the freedom that comes from God's forgiveness. When we confess, we allow God to cleanse us, renewing our strength and rejuvenating our souls, turning our summer of despair into a season of refreshing hope.

**The Role of Forgiveness and Repentance in Unburdening Guilt**

Forgiveness is a powerful force that releases us from the chains of guilt. Forgiveness isn't always easy, though, especially when it comes to forgiving ourselves. The key to unburdening ourselves of guilt is understanding that forgiveness is not a feeling. It's a choice. It is deciding to let go of the resentment we hold against ourselves or others and choosing to walk in freedom.

Repentance, on the other hand, involves more than just feeling sorry for what we have done. It is a change of heart and mind that leads to a change in behavior. **Acts 3:19** encourages us to **"Repent, then, and turn to God, so that your sins may be wiped out, that times of refreshing may come from the Lord."** Repentance brings about a fresh start, an opportunity to leave behind what weighs us down and step into the grace and mercy that God offers.

> **Forgiveness is not a feeling; it's a choice.**

### The Story of Peter: A Disciple's Regret and Redemption

Peter, one of Jesus's closest disciples, intimately understood the weight of guilt.

Known for his impulsive nature and fervent loyalty, Peter boldly declared his unwavering commitment to Jesus, vowing that he would never abandon Him. However, when the pressure mounted, Peter's courage crumbled. In a moment of fear and weakness, he denied knowing Jesus three times. The moment the rooster crowed, the reality of his actions hit him like a tidal wave, and he was overwhelmed with remorse. The Gospel of Luke recounts, **"The Lord turned and looked straight at Peter. Then Peter remembered the word the Lord had spoken to him: 'Before the rooster crows today, you will disown me three times.' And he went outside and wept bitterly." (Luke 22:61-62, NIV)**.

Imagine the depths of Peter's despair at that moment. The shame of betrayal, the sorrow of lost loyalty, and the fear of losing his place among the disciples flooded his heart. Peter could have easily allowed this profound failure to define him, letting guilt overshadow his identity and mission. He might have hidden in the shadows, convinced that he was no longer worthy to follow Jesus or fulfill the call on his life.

Jesus, in His infinite grace, sought Peter out after His resurrection. He didn't abandon Peter to wallow in guilt. Instead, He provided an opportunity for redemption. In a powerful moment on the shore of the Sea of Galilee, Jesus asked Peter three times, **"Do you love me?" (John 21:15-17, NIV)**. This poignant exchange was more than just a reaffirmation of love. It was a profound act of restoration. Each question offered Peter a chance to confront his past, acknowledge his failures, and step into forgiveness.

Peter's response was not just an affirmation of love. It was a declaration of his willingness to be restored. Through this act, Jesus not only forgave Peter but also entrusted him with a renewed purpose: **"Feed my sheep."** Peter's journey from guilt to redemption was complete, transforming him into a foundational leader of the early church. He went on to preach boldly, heal the sick, and lead many to faith, embodying the grace and power of the Gospel he once feared he had betrayed.

Peter's story reminds us that no matter how deep our guilt may run, God's grace runs deeper still. We, too, can find healing and redemption in the face of our failures. God does not define us by our past mistakes but rather invites us to embrace His forgiveness and walk in the newness of life He offers. Like Peter, we can rise from our regrets and step into the calling God has placed on our lives, using our experiences to minister to others who may also be wrestling with guilt and shame.

Peter's journey from guilt to redemption serves as a profound reminder of God's grace and the possibility of restoration. Just as Peter chose to confront his feelings of inadequacy and shame, we too, are invited to take actionable steps toward healing our own relational baggage and unrepented sin. The journey toward healing may seem daunting, but it begins with the understanding that we are not defined by our past mistakes. Instead, we have the opportunity to embrace forgiveness and reconciliation.

As we reflect on Peter's transformation, moving from a moment of failure to a foundational role in the early church, we can see how God's grace can work in our lives. By taking practical steps to acknowledge our guilt, seek forgiveness, and accept God's grace, we can break free from the chains of regret that hold us back. The following steps will guide us in releasing guilt and moving toward a future filled with hope and purpose, just as Peter discovered after his encounter with the risen Christ.

**Practical Steps to Release Guilt**

1. **Acknowledge Your Guilt:** The first step to overcoming guilt is to admit that it exists. Take a moment to reflect on your feelings and recognize the specific actions or decisions that have led to this guilt. Being honest with yourself about what happened and how it impacted your life is crucial. Acknowledging your guilt allows you to understand its effects not only on your emotional well-being but also on your relationships with God and others. It's important to confront the uncomfortable feelings instead of burying them, as this sets the foundation for healing.

2. **Confess and Repent:** Once you have acknowledged your guilt, bring it before

God. Confess your sins honestly, laying bare your heart without minimizing or justifying your actions. This act of confession is about transparency and humility before God. Repentance involves not just seeking forgiveness but also making a conscious decision to turn away from the behaviors or actions that caused the guilt. Embrace the promise found in **1 John 1:9**: **"If we confess our sins, He is faithful and just and will forgive us our sins and purify us from all unrighteousness."** Remember, God is eager to forgive, and His grace covers all sin.

3. **Seek Reconciliation:** If your guilt involves another person, it's vital to take steps to make things right. This could mean reaching out to apologize, seeking forgiveness, or making restitution where applicable. Understand that reconciliation is a process that may take time, and the response of the other party may not always align with your hopes. However, what matters most is your willingness to take that initial step

toward healing. It demonstrates a commitment to restoring relationships and moving forward positively.

4. **Accept God's Forgiveness**: One of the most challenging aspects of releasing guilt can be forgiving ourselves. Accept that God's grace is sufficient for your shortcomings and that His forgiveness is complete. Trust in His promise that He has removed your sins **"as far as the east is from the west" (Psalm 103:12)**. Embrace the truth that you are not defined by your mistakes. Instead, you are a beloved child of God. This acceptance is essential for your healing journey, allowing you to move forward without the burden of guilt.

5. **Let Go and Move Forward:** Making the conscious choice to release guilt is crucial for your spiritual and emotional health. Refuse to dwell on past mistakes. Instead, focus on God's promises and His plans for your future. Surround yourself with a supportive community that encourages growth and healing. Engage with others who can uplift you,

share their experiences, and offer accountability. Consider joining a support group or seeking the guidance of a mentor who can help you navigate this journey. The goal is to transform your experience of guilt into a catalyst for growth, allowing you to step into the freedom that comes from living in God's grace.

**Your Invitation: Choose Freedom Over Guilt**

Guilt and unrepented sin can feel like chains around your soul, restricting your ability to experience the fullness of life that God intends for you. They weigh heavy on your heart, creating a burden that can overshadow your joy and peace, but here's the truth: You don't have to live under their weight. God offers a path to forgiveness, grace, and a fresh start, one that invites you to leave the past behind and embrace the abundant life He has for you.

The story of Peter illustrates this beautifully. After his moments of betrayal, he could have been defined by his failures, trapped in the cycle of guilt and shame. Instead, he chose to respond to God's call for reconciliation. Jesus reached out to him with love and forgiveness, providing an opportunity for Peter to affirm his commitment and find renewed purpose. This same invitation is extended to you today. No matter the depth of your guilt or the weight of your past, God is waiting with open arms, eager to wipe your slate clean and help you walk in freedom.

As you stand at the crossroads of guilt and grace, consider the power of choosing freedom. Freedom is not merely the absence of guilt. It is the presence of God's love and acceptance in your life. It's a decision to believe that your mistakes do not define you. **God's love does.**

Take the first step toward healing today. Acknowledge your feelings, confess your sins, and open your heart to God's transformative grace. Surround yourself with a community that encourages growth and supports your journey toward reconciliation. By doing so, you will experience the profound truth found in **1 John 1:9**: **"If we confess our sins, he is faithful and just and will forgive us our sins and purify us from all unrighteousness."**

As you embrace God's forgiveness, let go of the chains that bind you. Trust in His promise of restoration and allow His grace to wash over you, bringing peace to your heart and clarity to your mind. With each step you take towards freedom, you will discover the joy of living in alignment with your true identity as a beloved child of God.

Remember, choosing freedom over guilt is a daily decision, a commitment to live in the light of God's love and grace. Step forward with confidence and embrace the fresh start that God offers. The weight of guilt can be lifted, making way for a life marked by purpose, joy, and deep connection with God and others.

**Reflection Questions:**

- Are there any areas in your life where you are holding onto guilt?
- What steps can you take today to seek forgiveness from God or others?
- How can you embrace the freedom that comes from God's forgiveness?

**Action Steps:**

- **Write a Prayer of Confession:** Take a moment to write a heartfelt prayer, confessing any areas of guilt or unrepented sin. Ask God for His forgiveness and guidance.
- **Reach Out for Support:** Consider reaching out to a trusted friend, mentor, or pastor to share your burden and seek accountability.
- **Start a Forgiveness Journal:** Begin journaling about your journey toward forgiveness and healing. Reflect on God's promises and document the steps you are taking to release guilt and move forward.

# 9

# DEPRESSION'S HEAVY LOAD

**The Hidden Struggle**

Every day, Amanda put on her mask before heading out into the world. She was a successful professional, always dressed impeccably, and known for her cheerful demeanor and quick wit. On the outside, everything seemed perfect. She had a thriving career, a loving family, and an active social life. Inside, Amanda was fighting a battle no one could see.

Depression had crept into her life slowly, like a fog rolling in over a calm sea. At first, she just felt tired, more tired than usual. Then came the sleepless nights, the heaviness in her chest, the constant feeling that something was missing. She found herself dreading the start of each day, feeling overwhelmed by the simplest tasks, and losing interest in the things she once loved.

Amanda tried to ignore it, telling herself to snap out of it, to "just be happy." She feared that admitting her struggle would make her seem weak or ungrateful. She plastered on a smile, showed up to meetings, and attended social events, all while feeling like she was carrying a heavy weight on her shoulders that no one else could see. She felt isolated in her pain, convinced that no one would understand.

One day, Amanda's close friend, Jennifer, noticed that her laughter didn't reach her eyes anymore. She gently asked, "Are you okay? You don't seem like yourself." For a moment, Amanda considered brushing it off like she had done so many times before, but something in Jennifer's voice made her pause. She felt a lump in her throat as tears welled up in her eyes. "I'm not okay," she whispered, "I think I'm depressed, but I don't know how to get out of this."

**Exploring the Baggage of Depression**

Depression is a complex and often misunderstood condition that affects millions of people worldwide. It can manifest in many ways: persistent sadness, a lack of interest in activities, fatigue, feelings of hopelessness, or physical symptoms like headaches and stomach aches. It's a heavy burden, a weight that can make even the simplest of tasks feel like climbing a mountain.

The thing about depression is that it often doesn't look like what people expect. It doesn't always mean someone is crying in a dark room. Sometimes, it looks like Amanda, who was outwardly successful but inwardly struggling. Depression can be invisible, making it all the more isolating. It's a form of baggage that many carry in silence, fearing judgment or misunderstanding.

**Psalm 38:6** says, **"I am bowed down and brought very low; all day long I go about mourning."** This verse reflects the deep despair and sorrow that often accompany depression. It is a reminder that this is not a new struggle.

People have faced and battled these feelings throughout history.

## Understanding Depression's Roots

### The Despair of Jeremiah: A Reflection on Faith and Depression

Jeremiah, often called the "weeping prophet," is a poignant example of someone who wrestled profoundly with despair. The context of his lament in **Jeremiah 20:14**, where he cries out, **"Cursed be the day I was born! May the day my mother bore me not be blessed!"** reveals a heart weighed down by immense sorrow and frustration. Imagine the depth of despair that would lead him to utter such words. He was tasked with delivering a message of impending judgment to a people who largely rejected him, facing constant opposition, ridicule, and isolation. The emotional toll of being a prophet in such a tumultuous time, coupled with the burden of witnessing his nation's moral decline, surely left him feeling crushed and desolate.

Jeremiah's lament is not just a moment of weakness. It is a raw, honest expression of his suffering. His feelings resonate with many who find themselves grappling with depression. This biblical account reminds us that experiencing deep sadness or despair is a part of the human condition, even for those with unwavering faith. It illustrates that faith does not exempt us from the trials of life, nor does it negate the reality of our struggles. In fact, it can often coexist alongside them, creating a complex tapestry of emotions that needs acknowledgment and understanding.

As we transition from Jeremiah's profound despair to practical strategies for managing depression, it's essential to recognize that addressing this condition requires a multi-faceted approach. Depression can have many roots: biological, psychological, social, or spiritual. It can result from trauma, loss, chronic stress, or chemical imbalances in the brain. While it's vital to understand that depression is not a sign of weakness or a lack of faith, it is equally important to recognize that it requires attention, compassion, and often professional help.

In the following section, we will explore effective strategies for managing depression that honor both our emotional struggles and our faith. These strategies can help create pathways to healing and restoration, offering practical steps to navigate through the shadows of despair toward the light of hope and renewal.

**Strategies and Resources for Managing Depression**

1. **Seek Professional Help:** Depression is not something you have to fight alone. Seek out a mental health professional, a counselor, psychologist, or psychiatrist, who can provide guidance, support, and, if necessary, medication. There's no shame in needing help. It's a courageous step toward healing.

2. **Build a Support Network:** Reach out to trusted friends, family, or a faith community. Share your struggles with those who care about you and are willing to walk alongside you. Isolation can worsen depression, but connection and

community can provide comfort and strength.

3. **Practice Self-Care:** Pay attention to your physical health. Exercise regularly, eat balanced meals, and get enough sleep. Engage in activities that bring you joy and peace, whether it's reading, gardening, painting, or simply taking a walk in nature. I struggle in this area just due to my schedule and choices, but when I am at my healthiest, I am out on the water or out running. Whatever it is, find your healthy rhythm.

4. **Ground Yourself in God's Word:** When depression clouds your thoughts, turn to Scripture for comfort and reassurance. **Psalm 34:17-18** says, **"The righteous cry out, and the Lord hears them; he delivers them from all their troubles. The Lord is close to the brokenhearted and saves those who are crushed in spirit."** This is one of my favorite verses in scripture. These words remind us that God is near, even in our darkest moments. This is a great verse to memorize, write down, and put

in places that you will see regularly, especially when you're struggling.

5. **Incorporate Prayer and Meditation:** Spend time in prayer, sharing your heart with God. Meditate on His promises and His love for you. Remember that God sees your pain, understands your struggles, and cares deeply for you. **1 Peter 5:7** encourages us to **"Cast all your anxiety on him because he cares for you."**

> **Remember that God sees your pain, understands your struggles, and cares deeply for you.**

6. **Consider Counseling or Support Groups:** Sometimes, talking to a professional or joining a support group with others who understand what you're going through can be incredibly healing. It creates a safe space to share, process, and find hope together.

**Stories of Overcoming Depression**

**The Story of Elijah: A Prophet's Despair**

Elijah, one of the most revered prophets in the Bible, is a compelling figure whose experience with despair can resonate deeply with anyone who has faced overwhelming challenges. After triumphing over the prophets of Baal on Mount Carmel, where he called down fire from heaven, Elijah should have been riding high on the waves of victory and vindication. Instead, he found himself in a harrowing state of fear and anxiety when Queen Jezebel vowed to take his life. The dramatic shift from victory to peril is striking and reveals the fragile nature of our emotional state.

In the face of such danger, Elijah fled into the wilderness, overwhelmed by exhaustion and despair. Picture him, weary and anxious, running away from the very people he had once boldly confronted. As he sat under a broom bush, he prayed, **"I have had enough, Lord. Take my life; I am no better than my ancestors" (1 Kings 19:4)**. These words express a depth of despair that many can relate to, feeling like you've reached your breaking point, believing that your efforts have been futile, and longing for relief from the weight of despair.

Imagine the loneliness Elijah felt at that moment. He had just faced hundreds of prophets and fought for the honor of God, and yet now he was alone, hiding in a barren wilderness. The juxtaposition of his earlier triumph and his current desolation highlights the emotional rollercoaster that many experience. The mental toll of battling fear, isolation, and exhaustion can lead to feelings of inadequacy and hopelessness, even for those who have experienced God's miraculous power.

God's response to Elijah is nothing short of compassionate. Rather than rebuke him for his fear, God provided sustenance in the form of food and water. He allowed Elijah to rest and recuperate before encouraging him to continue on his journey. This gentle care is a profound reminder that God meets us in our lowest moments, offering the support and strength we need to rise again. He reassured Elijah that he was not alone and that there was still purpose in his life.

Elijah's story encourages us to acknowledge our struggles and seek help during times of despair. It illustrates that even the most faithful servants of God can encounter deep emotional challenges, but with God's nurturing presence, healing and renewal are possible. Just as God fed Elijah physically and spiritually, He provides for us, reminding us that, in our darkest moments, we can find hope and direction.

As we transition to exploring practical strategies for managing depression, we can draw inspiration from Elijah's journey. His experience shows us that it is essential to recognize our feelings, seek support, and allow God's grace to guide us through our struggles. By doing so, we open ourselves to healing and the possibility of transformation, just as Elijah did after receiving God's nurturing care.

**Practical Steps to Lighten the Load**

1. **Acknowledge Your Feelings:** It's essential to give yourself permission to feel whatever emotions arise during difficult times. Suppressing or ignoring

your feelings can lead to an emotional backlog that eventually becomes overwhelming. Take time to acknowledge what you're feeling, whether it's sadness, anger, frustration, or fear. Consider writing your feelings down in a journal or discussing them with a trusted friend or counselor. This act of acknowledgment is not only a first step toward processing your emotions but also a way to validate your experiences, making it easier to navigate the complexities of your mental state.

2. **Seek Help Early:** Recognizing the signs of depression and seeking help promptly can make a significant difference in your journey toward healing. Don't wait until you feel completely overwhelmed before reaching out. Whether it's a doctor, counselor, or a pastor, early intervention can help address the underlying issues before they escalate. Professional support can provide you with coping strategies, resources, and a safe space to explore your feelings, setting a solid foundation for recovery.

3. **Cultivate a Daily Routine:** Creating a structured daily routine can help bring a sense of stability and normalcy to your life. When you're feeling low, it's easy to lose track of time and slip into unhealthy habits. A routine that incorporates time for work, relaxation, and social interaction can foster a sense of purpose and direction. Consider scheduling small tasks that you can accomplish each day, even if they're minor. This structure not only keeps you engaged but also provides measurable achievements that can boost your mood and motivation.

4. **Engage in Regular Physical Activity:** Physical activity is a powerful antidote to depression. Exercise releases endorphins, often referred to as the body's natural mood lifters, which can help reduce feelings of sadness and anxiety. You don't need to engage in intense workouts. Even a short walk outside can refresh your mind and body. Aim to incorporate movement into your daily routine, whether it's stretching, yoga, or

a stroll in the park. Finding activities you enjoy can make this step feel less like a chore and more like a way to nourish yourself.

5. **Practice Gratitude:** In moments of darkness, it's easy to focus solely on what's wrong. Practicing gratitude shifts your perspective and helps you appreciate the positives in your life, no matter how small they may seem. Start by keeping a gratitude journal where you write down three things you are thankful for each day. This simple practice can have a profound impact on your mental health, encouraging a mindset of abundance rather than scarcity. Over time, you may find that acknowledging the good in your life becomes a natural habit that uplifts your spirit.

6. **Lean into Your Faith:** Your faith can be a powerful source of strength and comfort during times of depression. Trust that God is with you in your battle, providing the support you need to navigate this challenging journey. Lean into your relationship with Him through

prayer, meditation, or reading Scripture. Remember that His grace is sufficient, and His power is made perfect in your weakness, as stated in **2 Corinthians 12:9**. Allow your faith to guide you, offering reassurance that you are not alone and that healing is possible with God's help. Connecting with your faith community can also provide additional support and encouragement as you work through your feelings.

**Your Invitation: Embrace Hope Amidst the Darkness**

Depression may feel like a heavy load, a weight that seems insurmountable, but it's essential to remember that you are not meant to carry this burden alone. The reality of mental health struggles can often lead us to feel isolated, as if we are the only ones grappling with the shadows. However, there is hope, healing, and freedom available to you. God sees your struggle. He knows your pain and walks beside you, ready to lift you up and carry you through the darkest moments.

In times of despair, it can be hard to envision a path forward. However, it is crucial to take the first step. This means reaching out, whether to a trusted friend, a counselor, or a pastor. Sharing your burdens can be incredibly freeing and can provide you with the support you need to navigate through the storm. Remember, it's okay to seek help. It is a sign of strength, not weakness.

Additionally, I want to recommend a powerful resource that has been a source of encouragement for many, including myself: *Hope in the Dark* by Craig Groeschel. This book delves into the complexities of faith amidst struggles and challenges, offering profound insights into how we can find hope even when circumstances feel bleak. Groeschel shares relatable stories and biblical truths that remind us of God's presence and promises, emphasizing that, even in our darkest valleys, His light can guide us home.

As you embark on this journey towards healing, trust that God's grace will be sufficient for you. Just as He walked with figures like David and Elijah, He will walk with you. Lean into His presence and allow His light to penetrate the shadows of despair. Embrace the truth that you are never alone. God's love is a beacon of hope that can illuminate the path ahead.

> **Healing is a process, and it's okay to take it one day at a time.**

Let today be a turning point. Allow hope to fill your heart and take confident steps toward a brighter future. Remember, healing is a process, and it's okay to take it one day at a time. As you reach out for help and explore resources like *Hope in the Dark*, know that God is ready to transform your pain into purpose and guide you toward the abundant life He desires for you. Embrace hope amidst the darkness, for it is through this journey that you will discover the beauty of resilience, healing, and renewed faith.

**Reflection Questions:**

- What steps can you take today to address any feelings of depression or anxiety you may have?
- How can you lean on your faith to help you through these difficult times?
- Who in your life can you reach out to for support and encouragement?

**Action Steps:**

- **Reach Out:** Make a call or send a message to a trusted friend, counselor, or pastor to start a conversation about what you're feeling.
- **Start a Gratitude Journal:** Begin writing down three things you are grateful for every day to help shift your focus from pain to praise.
- **Practice Self-Care:** Set aside time for activities that nurture your body, mind, and spirit.

# 10

## THE JOURNEY OF ACKNOWLEDGMENT

**The Power of Naming Your Baggage**

Mark had always been a perfectionist. Growing up, he was the straight-A student, the star athlete, the one everyone turned to for help. On the outside, his life looked flawless: a beautiful family, a successful career, a nice house in a friendly neighborhood. Inside, though, Mark was struggling. He felt a constant weight on his chest, a pressure that he couldn't explain. No matter how much he accomplished, it was never enough. He was exhausted, both physically and emotionally.

One night, after another argument with his wife about his long hours at work, Mark sat alone in his living room, his mind racing. He knew he wasn't just tired. Something deeper was at play. He remembered a conversation he had with a friend who suggested he try naming his baggage, giving a name to the specific things weighing him down.

At first, it felt silly, but as he thought about it, he realized he was carrying around more than just a busy schedule. He was lugging around expectations, expectations from his parents to be perfect, from society to succeed, from himself to never fail. He sat there, pen in hand, and wrote, "I am carrying the baggage of unrealistic expectations." Then another thought came, "I am carrying the weight of unresolved guilt." Before long, he had a list of things he had never consciously acknowledged.

That night, Mark felt a small sense of relief. For the first time, he had identified what had been weighing him down all these years. He knew it wouldn't all be fixed in a moment, but acknowledging it was the first step in his journey toward freedom.

**Deep Dive into Admission**

Acknowledging the baggage we carry can be a daunting task. It requires us to face parts of ourselves and our past that we might prefer to ignore or forget. However, the journey of acknowledgment is essential for healing. Just as Mark experienced, naming our baggage is like shining a light into a dark closet. It helps us see what's there and decide what needs to stay and what needs to go.

> **Naming our baggage is like shining a light into a dark closet. It helps us see what's there and decide what needs to stay and what needs to go.**

**Job 7:11** captures the heart of this process: **"Therefore I will not keep silent; I will speak out in the anguish of my spirit."** Naming our baggage is about giving voice to what has remained unspoken, bringing it into the open where it can no longer control us from the shadows.

### Why Acknowledgment Matters

Acknowledgment plays a critical role in addressing the burdens we carry. One of the most significant aspects of acknowledgment is that it breaks the cycle of denial. Denial is a powerful force that can lead us to believe that if we simply ignore a problem long enough, it will fade away. The reality is quite the opposite. Baggage doesn't vanish when left unchecked. It festers and grows, often complicating our emotional landscape even further. By choosing to acknowledge our struggles, we disrupt this cycle of pretense. We confront the uncomfortable truth that something is amiss, paving the way for genuine reflection and, ultimately, healing.

Moreover, acknowledgment validates our experiences. When we take the time to name our baggage, we affirm our feelings and experiences, essentially telling ourselves, "It's okay that I feel this way." This act of validation is crucial, as it helps us break free from the shame and guilt that often accompany our struggles. Recognizing that our feelings are legitimate and worthy of attention allows us to move forward, empowering us to face our challenges head-on rather than burying them under layers of denial.

Additionally, acknowledgment is the gateway to healing. By naming our baggage, we can start addressing it directly. It's akin to diagnosing an illness. Once we understand what's wrong, we can seek the appropriate treatment. This process not only involves acknowledging the pain we've experienced but also allows us to identify the root causes of our struggles. With this clarity, we can implement strategies to heal, seek support, and embark on a transformative journey toward wholeness. Ultimately, acknowledgment serves as a powerful catalyst for change, allowing us to reclaim our lives and move forward with renewed strength and purpose.

Now that we understand the importance of acknowledgment in breaking free from denial, validating our experiences, and facilitating healing, the next question arises:

**How do we effectively acknowledge our baggage?**

Taking that first step can often feel daunting, but it's essential for moving forward. In the following section, we will explore practical strategies for admission that can help you recognize and confront the burdens you carry. These steps will guide you in your journey toward healing and restoration, equipping you with the tools you need to embrace a healthier, more fulfilled life. Let's dive into these strategies that will empower you to acknowledge your struggles and begin the path to liberation.

**Strategies for Admission**

1. **Reflect Honestly:** Set aside some quiet time to genuinely reflect on your life. Create a peaceful environment where distractions are minimized, and ask yourself, "What am I carrying that I haven't acknowledged?" Without judgment or analysis, allow your thoughts to flow freely as you write down whatever comes to mind. This

exercise isn't about fixing anything just yet. It's solely about recognizing and seeing the burdens you carry. This initial step of self-reflection can be eye-opening and may help clarify what truly weighs on your heart and mind.

2. **Give a Name to Your Baggage:** After identifying the feelings, patterns, or experiences that are weighing you down, take the next step by giving them a name. This might look like writing, "I am carrying the baggage of fear of failure," or "I am holding on to the burden of shame." By naming these issues, you give them a form and a shape, something tangible that you can confront directly. This act of naming not only empowers you but also helps you begin to detach from the emotional weight these experiences carry.

3. **Speak It Aloud:** There is tremendous power in speaking your baggage out loud, whether it's to yourself, to God, or to someone you trust. Verbalizing the weight you carry can take immense courage, but doing so helps to break the

hold these feelings have over you. Bringing your burdens out of the darkness and into the light allows for healing and clarity. It transforms abstract feelings into concrete realities that you can address. Take a moment to say it out loud and feel the release that comes with that expression.

4. **Seek God's Perspective:** Once you have named your baggage, take the time to bring it before God in prayer. Ask Him to show you His perspective on what you are carrying. This is a pivotal moment where you can seek insight, wisdom, and courage to face what needs to be faced. Remember that God walks alongside you every step of the way. His strength is made perfect in your weakness **(2 Corinthians 12:9)**. Invite His light into your situation and trust that He can provide the guidance you need to navigate through your struggles.

5. **Share with a Trusted Person:** Consider sharing what you've discovered with a trusted friend, mentor, or counselor. Sometimes, simply speaking your burden

to another person can bring a sense of relief and clarity that is hard to achieve alone. Choose someone who will listen without judgment and offer encouragement and support. Their perspective can provide validation for your feelings and experiences, and their support can be invaluable as you work through your admission process.

6. **Document Your Journey:** Keeping a journal throughout this process can serve as a powerful tool for reflection and growth. Write about your feelings, the burdens you are naming, and your conversations with God. Documenting your journey not only helps clarify your thoughts but also allows you to track your progress over time. It provides an opportunity to revisit your feelings and acknowledge how you've moved forward or what still needs attention. This practice can lead to deeper insights and reinforce your commitment to facing and managing your baggage.

By implementing these strategies, you can create a solid foundation for acknowledging the burdens you carry, leading you toward healing and renewal.

**The Continuous Journey**

Acknowledgment isn't a one-time event. It's a continuous process. Life is dynamic, and as we navigate through various experiences, we may accumulate new baggage or find that old wounds resurface when we least expect them. Just as we regularly clean out our closets to make space for new things, we also need to revisit our internal baggage from time to time, ensuring that we don't allow it to clutter our hearts and minds.

The psalmist captures this need for introspection and divine assistance in **Psalm 139:23-24**, which states: **"Search me, God, and know my heart; test me and know my anxious thoughts. See if there is any offensive way in me, and lead me in the way everlasting."** This heartfelt prayer reflects a desire for self-examination, inviting God to probe the depths of our hearts and reveal any hidden burdens we may be carrying. The psalmist understood that true insight into one's self requires divine guidance and wisdom, emphasizing the importance of surrendering our innermost thoughts and feelings to God's care.

When the writer asks God to search and know his heart, he acknowledges that our understanding of ourselves can be clouded by denial, fear, or shame. It's easy to overlook our baggage or to minimize its impact on our lives. However, inviting God into this process allows for a transformative experience. The psalmist's prayer is not just about identifying what weighs us down. It's also a plea for God's leading toward healing and wholeness. The reference to being led "in the way everlasting" highlights the journey of faith, suggesting that God's path is one of continual growth, restoration, and, ultimately, freedom.

This scripture encourages us to approach our acknowledgment journey with openness and vulnerability. It reminds us that we are not alone in our struggles. God is intimately aware of our hearts and desires to help us navigate through the complexities of our emotions. By inviting Him into our process, we can find clarity and direction, leading us to a more profound sense of peace and purpose as we work through our baggage.

Just as we would seek guidance from a trusted friend or mentor when sorting through a cluttered closet, we can lean into God's wisdom and love as we examine our lives and release what no longer serves us. Embracing this continuous journey allows us to grow, heal, and step into the fullness of life God has in store for us.

As we recognize the importance of acknowledging our internal baggage and inviting God into our journey of self-examination, it becomes clear that this process is not just about understanding our struggles. It's also about taking actionable steps toward healing and growth. With God's guidance and our commitment to change, we can begin to navigate our way forward. In the next section, we will explore practical steps that can help you move beyond acknowledgment and into a place of transformation, allowing you to release the burdens you carry and embrace a renewed sense of purpose and freedom.

**Moving Forward: Practical Steps**

1. **Create a Regular Reflection Routine:** Establishing a consistent time for reflection is essential in your journey toward acknowledging and addressing your emotional baggage. Consider setting aside time each week or month dedicated solely to this practice. Use a journal to write down your thoughts, meditate on your feelings, or simply sit quietly with your mind to allow your emotions to surface. As you reflect, ask yourself questions like, "Is there anything new I need to acknowledge?" or "Are there old patterns or feelings I need to revisit?" This intentional time can help you gain clarity on what you are carrying and promote ongoing self-awareness.

2. **Celebrate Your Progress:** It's important to recognize and celebrate the steps you've already taken toward

healing and self-discovery. I don't think people celebrate enough. I think sometimes we feel strange celebrating overcoming, but that might be the best thing we can celebrate. Acknowledge your small victories. Each time you name a piece of baggage you've been carrying, confront a fear, or take a step closer to freedom, take a moment to celebrate. Reflect on your growth and progress rather than focusing solely on what remains to be done. Remember, this journey is not about achieving perfection. It's about making progress and recognizing that every effort counts in your path to healing.

3. **Stay Connected to Your Support System:** Maintaining connections with supportive friends, family members, or support groups is crucial. Isolation can amplify feelings of loneliness and make our burdens seem heavier. Reach out to those who uplift you and encourage honesty about your struggles. Share your experiences and emotions with trusted individuals who can provide empathy,

understanding, and perspective. Engaging with a community can help lighten your load and foster a sense of belonging, reminding you that you are not alone in your journey.

4. **Lean on Scripture and Prayer:** Regularly returning to the Bible for guidance, comfort, and encouragement is a vital aspect of moving forward. Scriptures can provide profound insights and peace, helping to ground you in your faith. Verses like **Philippians 4:6-7** remind us not to be anxious but to present our requests to God, assuring us that His peace will guard our hearts and minds. Incorporate prayer into your routine as a way to communicate with God, expressing your fears, doubts, and hopes. Seek His guidance in your journey, trusting that He is with you every step of the way.

5. **Set Realistic Goals:** As you move forward, it's beneficial to establish realistic, achievable goals related to your emotional health. Break down larger objectives into smaller, manageable

steps. For example, if you're working to address past baggage, you might set a goal to have a conversation with a trusted friend about your feelings or to write down your thoughts on a specific issue. These small goals can lead to significant progress and can help you feel accomplished as you check them off along the way.

6. **Incorporate Healthy Coping Mechanisms:** Explore and incorporate coping strategies that promote emotional well-being. This might include physical activities, creative outlets like art or music, or mindfulness practices such as yoga or deep-breathing exercises. Find what works best for you and make it a part of your daily or weekly routine. These healthy coping mechanisms can provide you with tools to navigate stress and anxiety while creating a positive impact on your mental health.

## The Story of King David: A Heart Continually Seeking God

King David stands out as one of the most significant figures in the Bible, embodying the complexity of human experience and the depth of divine grace. His life was marked by triumphs and failures, and throughout it all, he understood the importance of regularly acknowledging his burdens before God. In the Psalms, we see David continuously coming before the Lord, pouring out his heart, and confessing not only his sins but also his fears, anger, and doubts. He didn't wait for everything to feel perfect before speaking to God. Instead, he brought his raw emotions to the table, trusting that God would meet him in his vulnerability.

David's journey is a poignant reminder of the power of honesty and humility in our relationship with God. Despite being a man of great achievements, a skilled warrior, a beloved king, and a gifted musician, David also grappled with profound flaws. One of the most infamous moments in his life was his affair with Bathsheba, which led to an unplanned pregnancy and, ultimately, the tragic death of her husband, Uriah. Instead of confronting his mistakes openly, David initially tried to cover up his actions, attempting to hide the truth rather than seeking God's guidance. This moment of failure reveals the human tendency to shy away from vulnerability, especially when faced with the weight of our mistakes.

However, David's story didn't end in despair. After being confronted by the prophet Nathan, David was brought face-to-face with the reality of his sin. Rather than wallowing in shame or continuing to hide, he acknowledged his wrongdoing. In Psalm 51, we find his heartfelt cry for mercy, a powerful expression of repentance: **"Have mercy on me, O God, according to your unfailing love; according to your great compassion blot out my transgressions" (Psalm 51:1, NIV)**. This psalm illustrates David's willingness to lay bare his heart before God, fully aware of his flaws and failures yet still trusting in God's grace and forgiveness.

David's life is a testament to the notion that it's not about achieving perfection but about cultivating a humble heart. His continual acknowledgment of his burdens allowed him to grow closer to God, transforming his mistakes into moments of deep connection with the Divine. He is remembered as "a man after God's own heart," not because he was flawless but because he was willing to admit his need for God's grace and guidance.

Through David's example, we are encouraged to embrace our imperfections and bring our struggles to God. Acknowledgment of our burdens, just like David did, opens the door for healing and restoration. It reminds us that our relationship with God can thrive even amidst our deepest flaws and that honesty before Him can lead to profound grace and transformation.

**Final Reflection: Keep Naming, Keep Moving**

> The journey of acknowledgment is not merely a destination but an ongoing process, a continual unfolding of the heart.

The journey of acknowledgment is not merely a destination but an ongoing process, a continual unfolding of the heart. Each step you take toward naming your baggage, whether it be fear, shame, regret, or any other weight you carry, brings you closer to the freedom that God desires for you. Acknowledgment is the first key to unlocking the door to healing. It invites you to confront your struggles with honesty and humility.

As you navigate this path, remember that God walks with you every step of the way. He sees your burdens and hears your cries, offering you comfort and strength when the load feels too heavy to bear. In the moments of doubt and despair, lean into His presence and trust that He longs to set you free from the chains of your past. Just as He was there for David and Jeremiah, guiding them through their struggles, He is present with you in your journey.

Each time you name a piece of baggage, you create a space for God's grace to work in your life. Acknowledgment helps you release the shame that often keeps you trapped in silence. It's a powerful act of vulnerability that can lead to profound transformation. Don't shy away from this practice. Instead, embrace it as a sacred opportunity to grow closer to God and deeper in your understanding of yourself.

Keep moving forward. The road to freedom may have its ups and downs, but every step counts. Whether you're revisiting old burdens or recognizing new ones, allow yourself the grace to process without judgment. Surround yourself with a supportive community that encourages your journey, and don't hesitate to seek help when needed. Remember, the act of naming your struggles is an invitation to God to enter into those places and bring healing.

As you continue this journey, hold fast to the promise found in **Philippians 1:6**, which assures us, **"He who began a good work in you will carry it on to completion until the day of Christ Jesus."** Trust that your story is still being written, and each acknowledgment brings you closer to the freedom and joy that God has in store for you.

Keep naming, keep moving, and keep trusting. The light of hope is just ahead, waiting to illuminate the path toward healing, renewal, and a life lived fully in the grace of God.

**Reflection Questions:**

- What baggage have you identified in your life that needs acknowledgment?
- How can you name your baggage in a way that feels meaningful and empowering to you?
- Who can you trust to share your journey with?

**Action Steps:**

- **Make a List:** Write down the pieces of baggage you've identified. Give them names and see them for what they are.
- **Share Your Story:** Choose a trusted friend or mentor to share your journey of acknowledgment with.
- **Pray and Reflect:** Use **Psalm 139:23-24** as a daily prayer to invite God into your process of acknowledgment and healing.

**The Power of Small Steps**

Sometimes, the journey of acknowledgment can feel overwhelming. There may be moments when the weight of what you're carrying seems too heavy to bear. In those moments, remember the power of small steps. You don't have to solve everything at once.

# 11

## THE BAGGAGE WE CAN'T LET GO

### The Unseen Weight

Imagine carrying a backpack that never seems to get lighter, no matter how far you walk or how hard you try to empty it. That was the experience of Jennifer, a woman who had been through more than her fair share of difficulties. Jennifer had grown up in a home where love was conditional, success was expected, and mistakes were unforgivable. As an adult, she carried the weight of those expectations, dragging it behind her like a heavy chain.

Jennifer excelled in her career, always striving to prove she was enough, yet she never felt satisfied. Even after achieving everything, she thought would bring her peace, a great job, a nice home, and financial security, she found herself waking up in the middle of the night, her heart pounding, a sense of dread sitting heavily on her chest. She felt like she was stuck, unable to move forward, like she was carrying a weight she couldn't see but could certainly feel.

It wasn't until a friend asked her a simple question, "What is it that you can't let go of?" that Jennifer began to realize she was still holding onto the belief that she was only as good as her last accomplishment. The baggage of her past expectations had stayed with her, silently sabotaging her joy and peace. For Jennifer, the first step was recognizing that there were things she was refusing to release, baggage that was not only unnecessary but harmful.

**Understanding Persistent Baggage**

We all have baggage that we struggle to let go of, baggage that we carry with us for years, even decades. This baggage could be unresolved pain, unfulfilled dreams, unmet expectations, or lingering guilt and shame. While some burdens are easier to identify and address, others persist, entrenching themselves deep within our hearts and minds. This persistent baggage often feels like an old friend, familiar, almost comforting in its predictability, even as it drains our energy and holds us back.

**2 Corinthians 10:5** reminds us of the power of confronting our thoughts and taking them captive: **"We demolish arguments and every pretension that sets itself up against the knowledge of God, and we take captive every thought to make it obedient to Christ."** Letting go of persistent baggage starts with identifying those thoughts and beliefs that have a stronghold in our lives and choosing to challenge them.

**Why We Hold on to Baggage**

One significant reason we hold on to baggage is the **comfort found in familiarity**. Even when the weight we carry is harmful, we often cling to it because it's what we know. The familiar patterns, thoughts, and feelings create a sense of security, even if that security is based on pain or discomfort. The unknown, on the other hand, can feel intimidating and frightening. Stepping away from persistent baggage means venturing into new territory, territory where we have to navigate our emotions, confront our past, and possibly face fears we've buried. This transition can be daunting, leading many to prefer the safety of the familiar, even when it is detrimental.

Another powerful reason we tend to hold on to our baggage is the **fear of vulnerability**. Releasing baggage requires us to open ourselves up in ways that can feel profoundly uncomfortable. It means admitting that we've been hurt, that we've made mistakes, or that we're not perfect. Vulnerability can feel akin to standing naked in a crowded room. It's an exposure that invites judgment and scrutiny. It is through this uncomfortable space of vulnerability that we can begin to experience genuine healing. While it may feel easier to maintain the façade of strength and control, true growth and restoration often emerge from embracing our vulnerabilities.

Finally, the **unconscious beliefs** we carry play a significant role in why we find it challenging to let go of baggage. Many of these beliefs were formed during our formative years and shaped by our families, culture, or society. They become so ingrained in our identity that we often do not recognize their presence. These beliefs can quietly influence our thoughts, behaviors, and decisions, making it difficult to break free from the patterns they create. By uncovering and addressing these unconscious beliefs, we can begin to dismantle the mental barriers that keep us tied to our baggage, allowing for deeper healing and transformation.

Understanding why we hold on to our baggage is crucial for moving forward. Recognizing the comfort of familiarity, confronting the fear of vulnerability, and unearthing unconscious beliefs are the first steps toward liberation from the emotional weights we carry. In the next section, we will explore practical steps for releasing this baggage and embracing a healthier, more fulfilling life.

**Practical Steps and Strategies for Moving Forward**

1. **Get Rid of Excuses (Luke 14:18-20):** One of the biggest barriers to letting go of persistent baggage is the excuses we make to keep it. We might say things

like, "I'm too busy," "It's just the way I am," or "I've tried before, and it didn't work." In **Luke 14:18-20**, Jesus tells the parable of a great banquet where the invited guests made excuses for not attending. One man said he had bought a field and needed to inspect it; another claimed he had just purchased five yoke of oxen and needed to test them. A third declared he had just gotten married and couldn't come. Each excuse caused them to miss out on a life-changing opportunity. Similarly, we often make excuses that prevent us from engaging in the hard work of letting go of our emotional burdens.

**Action Step***:* Make a list of the excuses you find yourself using regularly. Be honest with yourself and take time to reflect on their validity. Once you have them written down, commit to challenging each excuse with the truth of God's Word. For example, if you think, "I'm too busy," remind yourself that prioritizing your mental and emotional health is vital and deserves time. This process will help you recognize that these excuses are barriers, not truths, preventing your progress.

2. **Cut the Ties (1 Corinthians 15:33-34):** Persistent baggage often remains because we stay tied to the things that keep it alive: negative influences, toxic relationships, and old habits. **1 Corinthians 15:33-34 warns us, "Bad company corrupts good character."** To truly let go of what's holding us back, we may need to cut ties with people or situations that reinforce our baggage. This doesn't mean being harsh or unkind, but it does require discernment about who or what we allow in our lives.

**Action Step:** Identify any relationships, environments, or habits that contribute to your baggage. Consider making a plan to distance yourself or remove these negative influences from your life. This could mean setting boundaries with certain people, finding a new job, or changing your daily routine to include more positive influences. Surrounding yourself with supportive, uplifting individuals is essential for fostering a healthy mindset.

3. **Submit to God (James 4:7):** Letting go of baggage isn't just about removing the negative. It's also about submitting to the positive power of God. **James 4:7 reminds us, "Submit yourselves, then, to God. Resist the devil, and he will flee from you."** Submission involves surrendering our will to God's, trusting that He knows what's best for us and that He will help us let go of burdens that are too heavy to bear alone.

   **Action Step:** Spend time in prayer, asking God to help you release the baggage you're struggling with. Make it a daily habit to surrender your burdens to Him and ask for His strength to overcome. This practice can create a sense of peace and assurance, knowing that you are not alone in your struggles.

4. **Fill the Void (Romans 12:21):** When we let go of something, we create a void that must be filled. If we don't fill that void with something healthy, it can easily be replaced with something

equally or more damaging. **Romans 12:21 states, "Do not be overcome by evil, but overcome evil with good."** It's essential to replace negative thoughts and behaviors with God's promises, positive activities, and uplifting relationships.

**Action Step:** Make a list of activities, scriptures, and people that bring positivity and growth into your life. Whenever you feel the weight of your old baggage creeping back in, turn to these resources to fill the void. Engage in hobbies that uplift you, volunteer in your community, or read encouraging books. Surrounding yourself with positive influences can reinforce your commitment to moving forward.

**The Story of Job: A Testament to Perseverance and Determination**

The story of Job is one of the most profound narratives in the Bible, illustrating unwavering perseverance and determination in the face of extreme adversity. Job was a man of great integrity, described as "blameless" and "upright," who feared God and shunned evil (**Job 1:1**). He was blessed with a large family, immense wealth, and a life of prosperity. However, in a dramatic turn of events, Job's life was shattered by a series of devastating losses that would test his faith to its core.

One day, a heavenly council convened, and Satan challenged Job's righteousness, suggesting that he was faithful only because of the blessings he received. To demonstrate Job's true character, God allowed Satan to strip Job of everything he held dear. In a single day, Job lost his livestock, his servants, and, most heartbreakingly, all of his children in a tragic accident. In the midst of this unimaginable grief, Job's response was remarkable: **"The Lord gave, and the Lord has taken away; may the name of the Lord be praised" (Job 1:21, NIV).**

Despite his deep sorrow, Job did not curse God. Instead, he continued to worship Him. However, his trials were far from over. Satan then afflicted Job with painful sores all over his body, leaving him in physical agony. In his distress, Job's wife urged him to "curse God and die," reflecting the despair that enveloped their lives (**Job 2:9**). Job responded with strength: **"Shall we accept good from God, and not trouble?" (Job 2:10, NIV)**.

Job's friends, Eliphaz, Bildad, and Zophar, came to comfort him, but their attempts soon turned into accusations, suggesting that Job must have sinned to deserve such punishment. They believed that suffering was a direct result of wrongdoing. Job, feeling increasingly isolated, passionately defended his integrity, asserting his innocence while grappling with the weight of his suffering.

Throughout the book, Job engages in profound conversations with God, expressing his confusion, pain, and longing for answers. He boldly questions why the righteous suffer while the wicked prosper, struggling to reconcile his faith in a just God with the harsh reality of his circumstances. Job's vulnerability in these moments is striking. He does not shy away from expressing his anguish, illustrating the importance of honesty in our relationship with God.

Ultimately, God responded to Job, not with explanations but with reminders of His sovereignty and the mysteries of creation. In Job 38, God asks Job a series of questions that highlight the vastness of His wisdom and power, reminding Job of his place in the grand scheme of things. Job's response is one of humility and surrender: **"I know that you can do all things; no purpose of yours can be thwarted" (Job 42:2, NIV)**.

In the end, God restored Job's fortunes, blessing him with even greater prosperity than before. Job received back double what he had lost and was blessed with a new family and a long life. His story serves as a powerful reminder that even in the depths of despair, perseverance and faith can lead to restoration.

Job's journey teaches us the value of holding onto our faith, even when the world seems to be falling apart. His story encourages us to bring our questions and struggles before God, trusting that He sees our pain and desires to walk alongside us through our trials. In doing so, we can find strength, hope, and, ultimately, a renewed sense of purpose as we navigate our own challenges.

Job's unwavering faith amidst suffering invites us to reflect on our burdens and reminds us that acknowledgment and perseverance are vital steps in the journey of healing and restoration. His life exemplifies the profound truth that even when we cannot understand our circumstances, we can continue to seek God and trust in His goodness.

**Final Reflections: Freedom Awaits**

Letting go of persistent baggage isn't merely a challenge. It's an essential journey toward the abundant life that God desires for each of us. The process of releasing the weights that have held us back involves several critical steps. First, we must **acknowledge the baggage** we carry, recognizing not only what it is but also why it persists in our lives. This acknowledgment is the foundation of healing, as it brings our struggles into the light, allowing us to confront them directly.

Next, it's crucial to **identify the root** of our burdens. By understanding the beliefs, fears, or past experiences that cause us to hold on, we gain insight into the deeper issues at play. This understanding empowers us to take action.

As we navigate the journey of letting go, we can implement the **practical strategies** we've discussed, such as getting rid of excuses, cutting ties with toxic influences, submitting our struggles to God, and intentionally **filling the void** with positive influences. Each of these steps contributes to the process of release, guiding us toward a lighter, more purposeful existence.

Celebration is also a vital part of this journey. **Celebrate every victory**, no matter how small. Each time you release a piece of baggage, take a moment to acknowledge the progress you've made. Remember, I've emphasized the importance of this practice throughout our exploration because recognizing our advancements is crucial to maintaining momentum. Every step forward, no matter how minor, is worthy of celebration and gratitude.

Lastly, it's important to **keep going**. Letting go is not a one-time event. It's an ongoing process that requires patience and perseverance. Trust that God is at work within you, even when the results are not immediately visible. Every day presents an opportunity to release a little more, trust a little deeper, and experience the joy of living unburdened.

In this journey of acknowledgment and letting go, remember that freedom awaits. God longs to see you step into a life filled with hope, joy, and purpose. As you walk this path, lean into His promises and grace, knowing that He is committed to your healing. Embrace the process, and trust that each effort you make brings you closer to the abundant life He has prepared for you.

> **Letting go of persistent baggage isn't merely a challenge. It's an essential journey toward the abundant life that God desires for each of us.**

**Reflection Questions:**

- What is one piece of persistent baggage that you are still carrying?
- Why do you think you are holding onto it?
- What step can you take today to begin releasing it?

**Action Steps:**

- **Pray for Strength:** Ask God for the strength and wisdom to identify and let go of persistent baggage in your life. Invite Him into your process, asking for guidance and clarity as you begin this journey.
- **Identify the Baggage:** Take time to reflect on what specific burdens you are carrying. Write them down, and be honest with yourself about how they affect your life and relationships.
- **Explore the Roots:** Dig deeper into why you hold on to this baggage. Consider any underlying beliefs or fears that contribute to your attachment. Understanding the roots can empower

you to take the necessary steps to release them.

- **Take Practical Steps**: Implement the strategies discussed earlier, such as challenging excuses, cutting ties with negative influences, and actively seeking God's perspective through prayer and Scripture.

- **Share Your Journey:** Find a trusted friend, mentor, or counselor to share your struggles with. Speaking about your baggage can provide relief and accountability as you work towards letting go.

- **Celebrate Small Victories:** Have I mentioned you should celebrate? As you make progress in releasing your baggage, take time to celebrate each step forward. Acknowledge your efforts, no matter how small, as significant milestones on your path to freedom.

- **Stay Committed:** Remember that the process of letting go is ongoing. Make a commitment to regularly revisit your baggage, reflect on your progress, and continue seeking God's help along the way.

# 12

## CELEBRATE RECOVERY: A JOURNEY OF HEALING

Heads up! This chapter takes a different approach, and you might feel tempted to skip it. I understand. Sometimes, the topics we least want to confront are the ones that hold the most potential for growth. You can choose to bypass it, but I urge you not to. This chapter may resonate deeply with your own experiences, or it might equip you with insights that can help someone else in their journey. I genuinely believe in the transformative power of the principles we're about to explore, as I have witnessed them change countless lives for the better. Let's dive in together and talk about Celebrate Recovery!

## The Power of a Safe Place

Michael sat in the parking lot, his hands gripping the steering wheel tightly. He wasn't sure if he could go in. His heart pounded, and his mind raced with doubts. "What if they judge me? What if they see right through me? What if I'm too broken?" For years, Michael had tried to handle his pain on his own. He kept telling himself he was fine, that he could fix things, that he just needed more time and more willpower, but nothing had changed. In fact, things had only gotten worse.

A friend had told him about Celebrate Recovery, a group that met at a local church every Sunday night. At first, he resisted. The thought of sharing his struggles with strangers felt like too much. Deep down, though, he knew he needed help. He needed a safe place where he could be real, where he could be honest about the things he had been hiding, so here he was, sitting in his car, battling the urge to drive away.

Taking a deep breath, Michael finally opened the car door and made his way inside. He was greeted with warm smiles and open hearts. As the meeting began, he listened to people share their stories, stories of pain, struggle, and, most importantly, healing. For the first time in a long time, Michael felt a spark of hope. Maybe, just maybe, he had found a place where he could begin to heal, too.

## Introduction to Celebrate Recovery and the 8 Recovery Principles

Celebrate Recovery (CR) is a Christ-centered recovery program designed to help people find freedom from their hurts, habits, and hang-ups. Founded by John Baker at Saddleback Church, CR has grown into a global movement that provides a safe space for people to face their struggles and start the journey of healing.

CR is based on the eight principles of recovery, which are derived from the Beatitudes in the Bible. These principles provide a framework for moving from denial to freedom, from brokenness to healing. At its core, Celebrate Recovery is about creating a safe and supportive community where people can be honest about their pain and begin the process of letting go of the baggage they have been carrying. Here are the 8 Principles:

## The 8 Recovery Principles: A Pathway to Healing

1. **Realize I'm not God (Matthew 5:3):** Recognize that we are powerless to control our tendencies to do the wrong thing and that our lives are unmanageable. This principle is about coming to the end of ourselves and acknowledging our need for God. It's the starting point for any healing journey.

2. **Earnestly believe that God exists (Matthew 5:4):** Understand that God exists, that we matter to Him, and that He has the power to help us recover. This step is about finding hope in God's love and recognizing that we are not alone in our struggles.

3. **Consciously choose to commit all my life to Christ's care and control (Matthew 5:5):** Make a decision to turn our lives and our wills over to the care of God. This principle is about surrender:

letting go of our need to control and allowing God to lead.

4. **Openly examine and confess my faults (Matthew 5:8):** Honestly examine our lives and confess our faults to ourselves, to God, and to someone we trust. This step involves transparency and vulnerability, which are crucial for true healing.

5. **Voluntarily submit to every change God wants to make (Matthew 5:6):** Submit to God's process, allowing Him to transform our hearts and minds. This principle is about being willing to change and inviting God to work in the deepest parts of our lives.

6. **Evaluate all my relationships (Matthew 5:7):** Offer forgiveness to those who have hurt us and make amends for harm we have done, except when doing so would harm them or others. This step involves seeking reconciliation and healing broken relationships.

7. **Reserve a daily time with God (Matthew 5:9):** Spend time with God daily for self-examination, Bible reading, and prayer in order to know God and His will for our lives and to gain the power to follow His will. This principle emphasizes the importance of maintaining a daily connection with God.

8. **Yield myself to God to be used to bring this Good News to others (Matthew 5:10):** Step out to share our recovery story with others and to give back. This final principle is about embracing the healing process and helping others who are on their own journeys.

## How Celebrate Recovery Can Help Unburden Life's Baggage

Celebrate Recovery provides a unique and supportive environment where individuals can find freedom from the burdens they carry. One of the most significant aspects of this program is its commitment to creating a safe community for honesty. In a world where many feel pressured to maintain a brave façade, CR encourages vulnerability and openness. Participants are invited to share their struggles without fear of judgment, fostering an atmosphere where honesty becomes the cornerstone of healing. This space allows individuals to confront their baggage head-on, leading to genuine breakthroughs.

Rooted in biblical truth, the eight principles of Celebrate Recovery offer a strong foundation for those seeking transformation. By aligning their recovery journey with God's Word, participants are not just pursuing healing from their emotional or relational wounds. They are also engaging in spiritual growth and maturity. This biblical framework provides a guiding light, illustrating that recovery is not solely about overcoming challenges but also about deepening one's relationship with God.

Moreover, accountability and support are integral to the Celebrate Recovery experience. The program emphasizes the importance of community, encouraging participants to connect with others who are on a similar healing journey. These relationships cultivate a network of support, where individuals can share their experiences, provide encouragement, and hold one another accountable. Knowing that others understand their struggles can make the path to recovery feel less daunting and more attainable.

Finally, Celebrate Recovery offers a pathway to freedom from shame and guilt, two burdens that many carry into the program. Through principles centered on confession, forgiveness, and reconciliation, participants can begin to release these heavy weights. They discover the liberating truth of God's grace, which allows them to let go of the past and embrace a hopeful future. By acknowledging their shortcomings and seeking forgiveness, individuals can find healing and peace, stepping into the abundant life that God has planned for them.

In summary, Celebrate Recovery serves as a powerful tool for unburdening life's baggage. With its emphasis on honesty, biblical principles, community support, and the release of shame and guilt, it offers a holistic approach to recovery that nurtures both the spirit and the soul.

## Testimonies and Stories of Recovery and Healing

### Lisa's Story: Finding Freedom from Addiction

Lisa grew up in a broken home where alcohol and drugs were common. As a teenager, she started drinking to numb the pain, which soon led to a full-blown addiction. By the time she was in her twenties, Lisa had lost everything: her job, her family, her dignity. One night, she hit rock bottom and decided to attend a Celebrate Recovery meeting.

At first, she was skeptical. Could a church program really help her? As she listened to others share their stories, she felt a glimmer of hope. Over time, Lisa worked through the 8 principles, admitting her struggles, seeking God's help, and rebuilding her relationships. Today, Lisa is sober, has restored her relationship with her family, and serves as a CR leader, helping others find the freedom she once thought was impossible.

**David's Story: Healing from Betrayal**

David had been married for fifteen years when he discovered his wife's affair. The betrayal left him shattered, struggling with anger, bitterness, and feelings of inadequacy. A friend invited him to a Celebrate Recovery group, and David reluctantly agreed to go.

Through CR, David learned to process his pain and to forgive. He realized that holding onto bitterness was only hurting himself. As he worked through the principles, he found peace and strength in his relationship with God. Today, David's marriage is on the path to healing, and he has become an advocate for others dealing with betrayal and broken trust.

How do we start this journey? Let me make it simple.

**The Healing Journey: A Step-by-Step Approach**

1. **Start Small:** The journey to recovery begins with one small step. Celebrate Recovery encourages people to start by admitting their struggles and attending a

meeting. No one is expected to be perfect. The first step is simply showing up.

2. **Work Through the Principles:** As participants work through the 8 principles, they gradually uncover the layers of their baggage, bringing them into the light where they can be addressed and healed. The principles provide a step-by-step approach that leads to deep, lasting change.

3. **Lean on the Community:** Recovery is not a solo journey. At CR, people find a community of others who understand, support, and encourage them. This community becomes a source of strength and accountability, helping participants stay on track even when the road gets tough.

4. **Celebrate the Victories:** Every small victory is worth celebrating. Celebrate Recovery encourages participants to acknowledge their progress and to celebrate what God is doing in their lives. This celebration reinforces the

truth that healing is possible and that freedom is attainable.

**Reflecting on the Journey of Healing**

As we draw this chapter to a close, it's important to remember the powerful truth found in **Galatians 6:2: "Carry each other's burdens, and in this way, you will fulfill the law of Christ."** This verse encapsulates the heart of Celebrate Recovery, where individuals come together to share their struggles and find the support they need to heal. It emphasizes the significance of community in our journeys, reminding us that we are not alone in our battles.

The road to freedom from life's baggage is undoubtedly challenging and filled with moments of doubt and difficulty. However, with God's grace and the unwavering support of a loving community, healing is not just a possibility. It's a promise. Celebrate Recovery serves as a beacon of hope, demonstrating that no matter how heavy the burden, how deep the pain, or how long the struggle, there is always a path forward. Every step taken in this journey is a step worth celebrating, as it brings us closer to the freedom and wholeness that God desires for each of us.

If you ever find yourself in Sarasota, FL, and are looking for a supportive environment to begin or continue your healing journey, I invite you to reach out to me. I would love to introduce you to my friends at Celebrate Recovery and walk alongside you as you take these important steps. Together, we can carry the burdens we face and support one another on the path to healing. Remember, you are not alone. There's a community ready to embrace you, uplift you, and help you find the freedom you seek.

# 13

## LIVING AND CELEBRATING FREEDOM

**The Joy of Letting Go**

Samantha always loved the idea of being free, free from worry, free from fear, and free from the expectations of others. However, for most of her life, freedom felt like a distant dream, something she read about in books or heard about in sermons but never truly experienced. She was the type who meticulously planned every detail, from her daily schedule to the grocery list, ensuring everything was in perfect order, but beneath the surface, Samantha was exhausted. Her life felt like a constant cycle of overthinking, anxiety, and regret.

One day, she attended a seminar on the concept of freedom and what it truly means to live free. The speaker challenged everyone in the audience to take a physical object that represented something they were holding onto, such as a worry, a fear, or a past mistake, and throw it into a large bin at the front of the room. As she watched people walk forward, one by one, and release their objects, Samantha hesitated. Could it really be that simple? Could letting go of a piece of baggage be as easy as dropping a rock into a bin?

As she thought about it, she realized that her constant worrying was like a heavy chain around her heart. She picked up a small stone and, with trembling hands, wrote the word "worry" on it. Taking a deep breath, she walked to the front and, with a quick prayer, dropped the stone into the bin. Instantly, she felt a surprising sense of lightness. It wasn't that all her worries vanished that day, but something changed inside her. She had taken a step toward letting go, and it felt like a taste of true freedom.

From that moment on, Samantha made a decision: she would live differently. She began each day with a prayer for peace, reminding herself of the freedom that was hers in Christ. She learned to choose joy over fear, trust over control, and grace over guilt. Her journey wasn't perfect, and there were days when old habits tried to creep back in, but Samantha was learning to live free, one day at a time. She discovered that freedom isn't just a destination. It's a way of life, a daily choice to let go and trust God.

## Celebrating Freedom: Embracing a New Way of Life

Freedom is more than a single act of letting go. It's a daily commitment to live in the lightness and joy that God offers. As believers, we are called not only to seek freedom but to celebrate it. **Galatians 5:1** reminds us, **"It is for freedom that Christ has set us free. Stand firm, then, and do not let yourselves be burdened again by a yoke of slavery."** This verse serves as a powerful reminder that freedom is both a gift and a responsibility, a daily invitation to live in the fullness of what Christ has accomplished for us.

### What Does It Mean to Live Free?

Living free is a transformative journey that encompasses several vital principles, each contributing to a fuller, more joyful life.

First and foremost, living free means **choosing joy**. Joy is not merely a fleeting emotion. It's an intentional decision to focus on God's goodness rather than our circumstances. When we let go of our baggage, we create the space necessary for joy to flourish in our lives. It's about finding delight in the small moments, whether that's savoring a morning cup of coffee, enjoying a heartfelt conversation with a friend, or taking a leisurely sunset walk. Embracing gratitude as a daily practice helps shift our perspective from what is lacking to recognizing the abundance that surrounds us. A practical way to cultivate this joy is to start a "Joy Journal," where you write down three things each day that brought you happiness. Over time, this practice can profoundly change how you view your life, reinforcing the idea that joy is always within reach.

Secondly, living freely involves **trusting God's plan**. Trust serves as the foundation of true freedom. When we trust that God is in control, even amidst chaos, we can surrender our worries, fears, and uncertainties to Him. Building this trust comes through cultivating a daily relationship with God through prayer, meditation, and immersion in His Word. As our trust grows, the burdens that once weighed us down begin to lose their power over us. A helpful tip is to pause and pray whenever you feel overwhelmed by fear or worry. Take a deep breath and consciously surrender the situation to God, reminding yourself of His promises, such as those found in **Romans 8:28: "And we know that in all things God works for the good of those who love him, who have been called according to his purpose."**

**Being fully present** is another crucial aspect of living free. Often, our baggage keeps us anchored in the past or anxious about the future, robbing us of the richness of the present moment. Living free means making a conscious choice to appreciate where we are right now, allowing us to experience life more fully. This practice encourages us to listen more intently, love more deeply, and notice the beauty in our everyday surroundings. To foster this mindfulness, take time each day to focus on the present. Whether you're eating, walking, or engaging in conversation, immerse yourself in that moment, noticing the details, colors, sounds, and tastes without judgment or distraction.

Additionally, living free means **forgiving both others and ourselves**. Forgiveness is essential for liberation. When we cling to grudges or refuse to forgive ourselves, we become chained to our past. It's crucial to understand that forgiveness is not about excusing bad behavior but about freeing ourselves from the burden of resentment. It is a conscious choice to release the hold that past hurts and mistakes have over us. A powerful exercise is to write a letter of forgiveness. Whether it's to someone who has wronged you or as a self-forgiveness exercise, the act of writing it down can be a significant step towards releasing pain and moving forward.

Lastly, living free means **embracing our true identity**. Our freedom is deeply rooted in our identity in Christ. Recognizing that we are loved, chosen, and accepted by God allows us to let go of the need to prove ourselves to others. Living authentically means understanding that our worth is not contingent upon our achievements or failures but is established by God's unconditional love. To reinforce this truth, speak affirmations over yourself daily. Use scriptures like **1 Peter 2:9: "But you are a chosen people, a royal priesthood, a holy nation, God's special possession."** Reminding yourself of who you are in Christ, especially on days when self-doubt creeps in, can significantly bolster your confidence and sense of purpose.

> **Living free is about actively choosing joy, trusting in God's plan, being present, practicing forgiveness, and embracing our true identity.**

In summary, living free is about actively choosing joy, trusting in God's plan, being present, practicing forgiveness, and embracing our true identity. Each of these elements interweaves to create a rich tapestry of freedom, inviting us to experience life fully and authentically.

As we explore what it means to live free, it's important to remember that freedom is not just a destination but a daily practice. By integrating these principles into our lives, we can cultivate a mindset that fosters ongoing growth and renewal. To help you on this journey, let's delve into practical steps that can guide you toward experiencing daily freedom. These actionable strategies will empower you to incorporate the concepts of joy, trust, presence, forgiveness, and identity into your everyday routine, leading you closer to the abundant life God has in store for you.

**Staying Free: Practical Steps for Daily Freedom**

1. **Stay Connected to God's Word:** Freedom is nurtured through a daily relationship with God. Make time to immerse yourself in Scripture, reminding yourself of God's promises and truths. Verses like **John 8:36: "So if the Son sets you free, you will be free indeed,"** serve as daily reminders that freedom is not something we earn but something we receive through Christ.

- **Practical Tip:** Set aside 10 to 15 minutes each day for quiet time with God. Read a passage of scripture, meditate on its meaning, and pray. Let this time ground you in God's truth and renew your mind.

2. **Practice Gratitude:** Gratitude is a powerful antidote to negativity. It shifts our focus from what we lack to what we have. Each day, make it a habit to reflect on the things you are thankful for. Gratitude opens our hearts to God's goodness and reinforces our sense of freedom.

    - **Practical Tip:** Create a gratitude jar. Each day, write down one thing you're grateful for on a small piece of paper and put it in the jar. At the end of the month, read through your notes and celebrate the blessings you have experienced.

3. **Release Control Through Prayer:** Control is an illusion that often keeps us from experiencing true freedom. When we try to control everything, we end up feeling more burdened. Instead, release your need for control to God through prayer. When you feel anxious or overwhelmed, pause and pray, surrendering your worries to Him.
   - **Practical Tip:** Develop a "Surrender Practice." At the start and end of each day, spend a few moments in prayer, releasing your worries, plans, and fears to God. Visualize yourself placing them at His feet and walking away lighter.
4. **Surround Yourself with a Supportive Community:** Freedom flourishes in community. Surround yourself with people who encourage and uplift you. Share your struggles, victories, and everything in between with trusted friends, mentors, or a small group. Let them remind you of God's truth and support you on your journey to living free.

- **Practical Tip:** Join or form a small group where you can share your journey, pray together, and encourage one another. Community provides accountability and helps reinforce the commitment to living a life of freedom.

5. **Celebrate the Small Wins:** In case you forgot about celebrating, don't wait for big moments to celebrate your freedom. Find joy in the small victories, every step you take toward healing, every day you choose peace over worry, every time you let go of a little more baggage. Celebrating these moments as markers of progress reinforces the journey of living free.

   - **Practical Tip:** Set milestones for yourself and reward your progress. This could be a special treat, a fun activity, or simply taking time to thank God for how far you've come. Make celebration a regular part of your journey.

## Living Fully: Embracing a Life Without Baggage

To live fully means to embrace life with all its beauty, messiness, and unpredictability. It invites us to be open to new experiences, take risks, and step out in faith. This journey is about recognizing that life is not merely a destination but a continuous unfolding, where freedom is something we practice daily.

Being open to new possibilities is a crucial aspect of living fully. Letting go of the baggage that weighs us down opens our eyes to fresh opportunities. It empowers us to take risks, explore new roles, and pursue dreams that we may have kept buried due to fear or self-doubt. When we shed the limitations of our past, we allow ourselves to be transformed by the possibilities that lie ahead. Living fully means embracing what God is doing in and through us, unearthing potential we may not have known existed.

Choosing faith over fear is another vital element of living a liberated life. Fear can act as a powerful anchor, keeping us tethered to our insecurities and hesitations. However, when we cultivate faith, we propel ourselves forward. Living fully involves trusting God enough to take steps of faith, even in uncertainty. It is the belief that God's plans for us are good, and He will guide us every step of the way. This trust allows us to break free from the confines of worry and step boldly into the future He has for us.

Reflecting God's love becomes a natural byproduct of living free. When we embrace our freedom, we reflect God's love to the world around us. Our lives transform into powerful testimonies of His grace, mercy, and transformative power. We are called to be lights in the world, to love boldly, and to serve others out of the abundance of the freedom we have received. As we engage with others from a place of wholeness, we create ripples of love and encouragement that can inspire change in the lives of those we encounter.

> **When we embrace our freedom, we reflect God's love to the world around us.**

**Reflection Questions**

- What are some new possibilities that you feel called to explore now that you are working toward living free?

- In what areas of your life do you need to choose faith over fear, trusting God's plans for you?

- How can you actively reflect God's love in your community and relationships as you embrace your freedom?

# 14

## FINAL REFLECTIONS AND CLOSING THOUGHTS

**Dinner with My Daughter: A Journey to Freedom**

Today, I had the opportunity to reflect on a poignant moment from my past with my daughter, Aubrie. It's hard to believe how quickly time has passed since those carefree days of her childhood, filled with laughter and the sweetness of simple joys. I can still vividly recall the afternoons we spent at our favorite burger shop in Bradenton, a cozy little place known for its unique burgers stuffed with peanut butter, which we would dip in syrup. Yes, it was as amazing as you may imagine. Each bite felt like a gift straight from the Lord's banquet table, and the family who owned the restaurant were cherished friends from my church.

One evening, when Aubrie was still quite young, we decided to indulge in one of our regular visits. As was customary, the owner came out to greet us with her warm smile, sharing a few light-hearted jokes and welcoming us like family. As we settled into our favorite booth, the waitress brought over a cup filled with used crayons and paper for coloring, a little touch that always delighted the kids.

That day, something was different. While Lory and I browsed the menu, trying to resist ordering the same thing we always did, I noticed that Aubrie sat quietly, her brow furrowed in disappointment. Concerned, I leaned in and asked, "What's wrong?" She looked at me with her big, sad eyes and said, "All the crayons are broken."

I glanced at the cup and realized she was right. A few crayons were completely snapped in half, and others were chipped and worn down, leaving them looking less than perfect. I imagined she was used to receiving fresh, unblemished crayons at other restaurants, and I could see how the sight of these broken ones could bring her down.

At that moment, I felt a surge of inspiration to show her that, despite their imperfections, those crayons could still create beautiful things. "Hey, Aubrie," I said, "let me show you something." I picked up a broken crayon and demonstrated how it still worked, coloring vibrant lines across the paper. I explained to her that just because they were broken didn't mean they couldn't still serve their purpose. "Broken crayons still color," I told her, and I could see a flicker of realization in her eyes.

Maybe you have heard that phrase before or have a similar story. That night, I got to live it out. That lesson from so many years ago has remained etched in my heart. I understood that, like those crayons, people often feel like they can no longer be used or that their dreams are out of reach due to the baggage they carry, be it past mistakes, disappointments, or struggles. God is in the business of redemption, continually transforming brokenness into beauty. Just as I showed Aubrie that those crayons could still create, we too, can recognize that our imperfections don't disqualify us from living out our God-given purpose.

Witnessing Aubrie's transition from sadness to joy reminded me of the importance of perspective. It's easy to get caught up in our brokenness, feeling like we can't contribute or be used for something great. God sees beyond our flaws and failures, offering us hope and the chance for renewal. Our past doesn't define us. Instead, it's an opportunity for God's grace to shine through, illuminating the path to our freedom.

Reflecting on this experience with Aubrie reinforces the truth that our baggage doesn't need to hold us back. Each of us has the capacity to color the world in our unique way, even if we feel broken. The journey toward freedom is about embracing our imperfections and trusting that God can redeem every part of our story.

You have the same opportunity to embrace freedom in your own life. It's important to remember that freedom isn't merely the absence of baggage. It's the presence of purpose, joy, and connection.

**A Call to Live in Freedom**

As we close this journey, let's reflect on the importance of living in freedom. Remember **Psalm 55:22: "Cast your cares on the Lord, and He will sustain you."** This verse encapsulates the essence of what it means to let go and trust in God's faithfulness.

I believe in you and your ability to find freedom. You have the strength within you to let go of what holds you back and to step boldly into the life God has designed for you. Imagine the weight lifting as you release those burdens, the joy that comes from living unencumbered, and the clarity you'll find in pursuing your purpose.

As you reflect on your journey, I can't wait to hear about the changes you've made and the freedom you've discovered. Remember, it's never too late to reclaim your life. You are capable of so much more than you realize, and freedom is waiting for you on the other side of your courage.

Remember, the journey doesn't end here. Freedom is something we grow into every day. Continue to seek God, surround yourself with a supportive community, and live boldly and authentically. Let your life be a testimony of what it means to live free.

> **Freedom isn't merely the absence of baggage; it's the presence of purpose, joy, and connection.**

### A Call to Live a Life Full of Possibility and Hope

As you move forward, embrace the freedom that is already yours in Christ. Don't let the baggage of your past, the fears of your future, or the expectations of others hold you back. Instead, step boldly into the life that God has for you, a life full of possibility, purpose, and hope.

**Celebrating the Journey Ahead**

Your journey to living free doesn't stop here. Keep moving forward, keep trusting, and keep celebrating every step. Remember, freedom is not a destination. It's a way of life, and in Christ, it's already yours.

Go ahead, celebrate your freedom. Live boldly, love deeply, and embrace the abundant life God has for you, unburdened and free.

> **Live boldly, love deeply, and embrace the abundant life God has for you, unburdened and free.**

**Reflection Questions:**

- What does freedom look like for you in your daily life?
- Are there areas where you still feel weighed down? What can you do to release those burdens?
- How can you celebrate the freedom you have in Christ today?

**Action Steps:**

- **Make a Freedom Plan:** Identify one area where you want to experience more freedom and create a plan to work toward it. Write down the steps you'll take, the people who will support you, and the scriptures that will guide you.
- **Start a Gratitude Journal:** Commit to writing down three things you're grateful for every day. Reflect on how gratitude shifts your mindset from burden to blessing.

- **Find a Freedom Partner:** Identify a trusted friend or mentor who can walk with you on your journey to living free. Meet regularly to share, encourage, and pray for each other.

# APPENDIX

## I AM LIST

I am a child of God.
**Romans 8:16; 1 John 3:1,2**
I am saved by grace through faith.
**Ephesians 2:8**
I am redeemed from the hand of the adversary.
**Psalms 107:2**
I am an heir of eternal life.
**1 John 5:11-12**
I am forgiven.
**Ephesians 1:7**
I am led by the Spirit of God.
**Romans 8:14**
I am a new creature.
**2 Corinthians 5:17**
I am redeemed from the curse of the law.
**Galatians 3:13**
I am carried through by God Himself.
**Isaiah 46:4**
I am strong in the Lord and in His mighty power.
**Ephesians 6:10**
I am living by faith and not by sight.
**2 Corinthians 5:7**

I am rescued from the dominion of darkness.
**Colossians 1:13**
I am justified.
**Romans 3:1**
I am an heir of God and a co-heir with Christ.
**Romans 8:17**
I am blessed with every spiritual blessing.
**Ephesians 1:3**
I am an overcomer by the blood of the Lamb and the word of my testimony.
**Revelation 12:11**
I am the light of the world.
**Matthew 5:14**
I am an imitator of God, as a beloved child, to walk in Jesus' love.
**Ephesians 5:1**
I am healed by His wounds.
**1 Peter 2:24**
I am being transformed by the renewing of my mind.
**Romans 12:2**
I am heir to the blessings of Abraham.
**Galatians 3:14**
I do all things through Christ who strengthens me.
**Philippians 4:13**
I am more than a conqueror. **Romans 8:37**

I am blameless and free from accusation.
**Colossians 1:22**
Christ, Himself, is in me.
**Colossians 1:27**
I am firmly rooted in Jesus, and I am being built up in Him.
**Colossians 2:7**
I have been made complete in Jesus.
**Colossians 2:10**
I have been spiritually circumcised; my old unregenerate nature has been removed.
**Colossians 2:10-13**
I have been buried, raised, and made alive in Jesus.
**Colossians 2:12,13**
I died with Christ, and I have been raised up with Christ. My life is now hidden with Christ in God. Christ is now my life.
**Colossians 3:1-3**
I am chosen of God, holy and dearly loved.
**Colossians 3:12; 1 Thessalonians 1:4**
I am a son of light and not of darkness. 1
**Thessalonians 5:5**
I have been given a spirit of power, love, and self-discipline.
**2 Timothy 1:7**

I have been saved and set apart according to God's doing. **2 Timothy 1:9**; **Titus 3:5**

Because I am sanctified and I am one with the Sanctifier, He is not ashamed to call me brother. **Hebrews 2:11**

I am a holy partaker of a heavenly calling. **Hebrews 3:1**

I have the right to come boldly before the Throne of God to find mercy and grace in time of need. **Hebrews 4:16**

I have been born again. **1 Peter 1:23**

I am a living stone, being built up as a spiritual house for a holy priesthood, to offer up spiritual sacrifices acceptable to God through Jesus Christ. **1 Peter 2:5**

I am a member of a chosen race, a royal priesthood, a holy nation, a people for God's own possession. **1 Peter 2:9,10**

I am an alien and a stranger. **1 Peter 2:11**

I am an enemy of the devil. **1 Peter 5:8**

I have been given exceedingly great and precious promises by God by which I am a

partaker of God's divine nature.
**2 Peter 1:4**
I am forgiven on account of Jesus' name.
**1 John 2:12**
I am anointed by God.
**1 John 2:27**
I am loved.
**1 John 4:10**
I have life.
**1 John 5:12**
I am born of God, and the evil one... the devil... cannot touch me.
**1 John 5:18**
I have been redeemed.
**Revelation 5:9**
My sinful nature, in Jesus, has been healed.
**Isaiah 53:5**
I am the salt of the earth.
**Matthew 5:13**
I am the light of the world.
**Matthew 5:14**
I am commissioned to make disciples.
**Matthew 28:19,20**
I am a child of God.
**John 1:12**
I have eternal life.
**John 3:16**

I have been given peace.
**John 14:27**
I am part of the true vine.
**John 15:1-5**
I am clean.
**John 15:3**
I am Jesus' friend.
**John 15:15**
I am chosen and appointed by Jesus to bear fruit.
**John 15:16**
I have been given glory, I am one with Jesus.
**John 17:22**
I have been justified.
**Romans 5:1**
I died with Christ and died to the power of sin's rule over my life.
**Romans 6:1-6**
I am a slave of righteousness.
**Romans 6:18**
I am free from sin and enslaved to God.
**Romans 6:22**
I am free from condemnation.
**Romans 8:1**
I am a son of God.
**Romans 8:14-15; Galatians 3:26; Galatians 4:6**

I am a joint heir with Christ.
**Romans 8:17**
I am more than a conqueror through Christ, who loves me.
**Romans 8:37**
I am given faith.
**Romans 12:3**
I have been sanctified and called to holiness.
**1 Corinthians 1:2**
I have been given grace.
**1 Corinthians 1:4**
I have been placed into Christ by God's doing.
**1 Corinthians 1:30**
I have received the Spirit of God into my life, that I might know the things given to me by God.
**1 Corinthians 2:12**
I have been given the mind of Christ.
**1 Corinthians 2:16**
I am a temple, a dwelling place of God. His Spirit and His Life dwell in me.
**1 Corinthians 3:16; 1 Corinthians 6:19**
I am united to the Lord, and I am one in spirit with Him.
**1 Corinthians 6:17**

I am bought with a price, I am not my own, I belong to God.
**1 Corinthians 6:19-20; 1 Corinthians 7:23**
I am called.
**1 Corinthians 7:17**
I am a member of Christ's body.
**1 Corinthians 12:27; Ephesians 5:30**
I am victorious.
**1 Corinthians 15:57**
I have been established, anointed, and sealed by God in Christ, and I have been given to the Holy Spirit as a pledge guaranteeing my inheritance to come.
**2 Corinthians 1:21; Ephesians 1:13-14**
I am led by God in Triumphal procession.
**2 Corinthians 2:14**
I am a fragrance of Christ to God among those who are being saved and among those who are perishing.
**2 Corinthians 2:15**
I am being changed into the likeness of Jesus.
**2 Corinthians 3:18**
I no longer alive for myself, but for He who died and rose again on my behalf.
**2 Corinthians 5:14-15**
I am a new creation.
**2 Corinthians 5:17**

I am reconciled to God, and I am a minister of reconciliation.
**2 Corinthians 5:18-19**
I have been made righteous.
**2 Corinthians 5:21**
I am well content with weaknesses, ...; for when I am weak, then I am strong.
**2 Corinthians 12:10**
I have been crucified with Christ, and it is no longer I who live, but Christ lives in me.
**Galatians 2:20**
I am a son of God through faith in Christ Jesus.
**Galatians 3:26**
I am Abraham's seed and heir of the promise from God.
**Galatians 3:29**
I am no longer a slave but a son; and if a son, then an heir through God.
**Galatians 4:6-7**
I am a saint.
**Ephesians 1:1; 1 Corinthians 1:2; Philippians 1:1; Colossians 1:2**
I am blessed with every spiritual blessing.
**Ephesians 1:3**

I was chosen in Him before the foundation of the world, that I would be holy and blameless before Him.
**Ephesians 1:4**
I am adopted as a son through Jesus Christ to Himself.
**Ephesians 1:5**
I am sealed in Him with the Holy Spirit of promise.
**Ephesians 1:13**
I am alive together with Christ.
**Ephesians 2:5**
I have been raised up with Him, and seated with Him in heaven.
**Ephesians 2:6**
I am His workmanship, created in Christ Jesus for good works.
**Ephesians 2:10**
I am a fellow citizen with the saints, and I am of God's household.
**Ephesians 2:19**
I have access in one Spirit to the Father.
**Ephesians 2:18**
I have boldness and confident access to God through faith in Him.
**Ephesians 3:12**

My citizenship is in heaven; seated with Him in the heavenly places in Christ Jesus.
**Philippians 3:20; Ephesians 2:6**
I am capable.
**Philippians 4:13**
I have been rescued from the domain of darkness and transferred to the kingdom of His beloved Son.
**Colossians 1:13**
I have been redeemed.
**Colossians 1:14**
I am better than I deserve.
**Psalm 103:10-12**

# ABOUT THE AUTHOR

**Dr. Nicholas Williams** is the Amazon bestselling author of *When Fear and Faith Collide*, a book that resonated deeply with readers, landing on the Amazon bestseller list within its first week of release. As the Lead Pastor at South Shore Community Church in Sarasota, Florida, Dr. Williams is passionate about sharing the transformative message of the gospel.

Dr. Williams holds a B.A., M.A.M., M.Div., and D.Min. from Luther Rice University. When he's not writing or leading his congregation, he enjoys traveling or being on the water with his wife, Lory, and their two children, Aubrie and Noah. You can learn more about his work and connect with him at www.nic-williams.com.

Made in the USA
Columbia, SC
26 January 2025

07b5752c-7fde-44af-8d67-6074d09919faR01